A Royal Palace in Wales
CAERNARFON

Charles Kightly

Foreword by His Royal Highness The Prince of Wales

Contents

Inside Front Cover: *This fourteenth-century manuscript illustration depicts Edward of Caernarfon (King Edward II) and Queen Isabella. Edward took his name from the castle where he was born and was the first English prince of Wales (By courtesy of the Governing Body of Christ Church, Oxford: Bodleian Ms. Christ Church 92, f. 4v).*

Right: *Edward of Caernarfon created prince of Wales by King Edward I, 1301 (By permission of the British Library, Cotton Ms. Nero D II, f.191v).*

First Published 1991

Editorial Production by David M. Robinson and Diane Williams
Design by Tom Morgan
Principal site photography by Mick Sharp

Typeset by Afal Typesetting
Printed in Great Britain by William Caple

ISBN 0 948329 80 7

KENSINGTON PALACE

'And he saw a great city at the mouth of the river, and in the city a great castle, and he saw many great towers of various colours on the castle'.

So runs 'The Dream of Macsen Wledig', one of the tales from the celebrated collection of Welsh legends called *The Mabinogion*. We, of course, know the great castle at the mouth of the River Seiont as Caernarfon — a magnificent medieval fortress-palace.

From the time the Romans first fortified this site on the edge of the Menai Strait, Caernarfon has played a central role in the history of Gwynedd and Wales. Today, its strength lies in its power to excite interest in a turbulent and often violent past; in its majesty as a masterpiece of medieval military architecture (now reflected in Caernarfon's status as a World Heritage Site); and in the way the castle draws people from many countries beyond Wales to a greater understanding of its history. My own Investiture there, in 1969, was but one in a long line of royal associations with the castle.

I feel sure that this handsome book will be a fitting chronicle of the great fortress-palace of Caernarfon.

Introduction

Caernarfon is probably the most famous castle in Wales, and rightly so. A medieval royal palace as well as an immensely strong and strikingly beautiful fortress, it was built by King Edward I on a site already hallowed by ancient legend, and became the birthplace of his son, the first English prince of Wales. Since then it has been inextricably connected with the royal family, a connection reinforced by the Investiture there in 1969 of His Royal Highness Prince Charles, the present prince of Wales.

This souvenir booklet seeks to introduce the castle, to enhance the enjoyment of a visit, and to broaden understanding of what the visitor has seen. Lavishly illustrated, it highlights some of the most important aspects of this royal palace in Wales, and chronicles the momentous events which have taken place there. Above all, it focuses on the people associated with Caernarfon down the centuries, from Roman emperors and Welsh heroes to every one of the English princes and princesses of Wales.

'And at the river mouth he could see a great castle, the fairest that mortal had ever seen...' Caernarfon Castle viewed across the River Seiont.

The Legend of Caernarfon

The Legend

'And then he dreamed a dream . . . And he saw a great city at the mouth of the river, and in the city a great castle, and he saw many great towers of various colours on the castle. And he saw a fleet at the mouth of the river . . . And amidst the fleet he saw a ship . . . He saw a bridge of walrus ivory from the ship to the land, and he thought how he came along the bridge onto the ship. A sail was hoisted on the ship, and away she went over sea and ocean'.

'He saw how he came to an island, the fairest in the whole world, and after he had traversed the island . . . he could see valleys and steeps and towering rocks, and a harsh rugged terrain . . . And from there he saw in the sea, facing that rugged land, an island. And between him and that island he saw a country whose plain was the length of its sea, its mountain the length of its woodland. And from that mountain he saw a river . . . And at the river mouth he could see a great castle, the fairest that mortal had ever seen, and the gate of the castle he saw open, and he came to the castle'.

'Inside the castle he saw a fair hall. The roof of the hall he thought to be all of gold; the side of the hall he thought to be of glittering stones . . . And at the foot of the hall pillar, he saw a hoary-headed man seated in a chair of ivory, with the images of two eagles in red gold thereon . . . And he saw a maiden sitting before him in a chair of red gold. No more than it would be easy to look on the sun when it is brightest, no easier would it be than that to look on her by reason of her excelling beauty . . . And the maiden arose to meet him from the chair of gold, and he threw his arms around the maiden's neck . . .'

But at that moment Macsen Wledig, emperor of Rome, was awakened by his guards. From then on he could do nothing but pine for love of the dream-maiden, 'but he knew not where in the world she was'. So he sent messengers to seek her in every corner of the world, and after a year they came to the Island of Britain, and to Snowdon on its western edge. Recognizing the rugged land of the emperor's dream, they pressed on until they saw the island of Môn (Anglesey) facing them, and stood on the coastal plain of Arfon — 'the land opposite Môn'. Here they saw Aber Seint, the dream castle at the mouth of the river Seiont, where Caernarfon now stands: entering it, they found all as the emperor had dreamed, and hailed the maiden as empress of Rome.

Then, galloping by day and night, they returned to tell their master of their discovery, and guided him back to Britain and the castle of Aber Seint. On the very day he arrived there he married the maiden — whose name was Elen, daughter of Eudaf — and soon afterwards he built her a new stronghold in Arfon, called in Welsh 'Y gaer yn arfon', or Caernarfon — 'the fortress in Arfon'. She, in turn, built great roads throughout Britain for his armies, gaining thereby the name of Elen Luyddog, Helen of the Legions. Macsen stayed in Britain with her, but after seven years of absence the Romans deposed him for a new emperor. Only with the help of the men of Britain, led by Elen's brothers, did he eventually recover his empire. Yet many of the Britons never returned home, for they settled in the European lands they had conquered, founding there the realm of Brittany.

A coin of the Roman Emperor Maximus, A.D. 383-88 — the 'Macsen Wledig — Prince Macsen' of the Mabinogion (By permission of the National Museum of Wales).

Fact and Fiction

So runs *The Dream of Macsen Wledig,* one of the tales from the collection of Welsh legends called *The Mabinogion.* Perhaps first written down in the eleventh century — though it may have been told much earlier — the tale combines romantic fiction with half-remembered fact. For Macsen Wledig ('Prince Macsen') was a real person. He is known to history as Magnus Maximus, a Spanish-born general who was proclaimed emperor in A.D. 383 by the Roman troops in Britain, and led them to a short-lived conquest of the western Roman empire before his defeat and execution in Yugoslavia five years later.

In his time, too, there really was a 'castle' at the mouth of the river Seiont: the Roman fort of *Segontium,* whose extensive remains can still be seen on the south-eastern outskirts of Caernarfon. Established in A.D. 77, during the final stages of the Roman conquest of Wales, it was eventually abandoned not long after Maximus's bid for power. Perhaps he really did take its garrison with him to Europe, for a few decades later the *Segontienses* — the regiment of *Segontium* — are recorded as palace guards in distant Yugoslavia, where they may have been stranded after his defeat. The mother church of Caernarfon, moreover, is dedicated to St Peblig or Publicius, reputed to have been one of Maximus's sons: standing by the Roman fort rather than in the medieval and later town, it may indeed mark the site of a church founded during the brief reign of Macsen Wledig.

Whether or not the Emperor Maximus actually had close personal links with the fort of *Segontium,* both he and it clearly made a deep impression on the folk-memory of north Wales. The stern-minded monk Gildas, writing in about 540, censored Maximus as a usurper who denuded Britain of troops for his conquests, thus exposing it to the ravages of Picts, Irishmen and Saxons. But to later poets (like the compiler of the *Dream of Macsen Wledig*) he was not only a national hero, but also the forefather of many of the princely families of Wales. The shadow of his fame still survives on the ninth-century Pillar of Eliseg, which stands near Valle Crucis Abbey by Llangollen: its time-worn inscription recorded 'Maximus the King, who killed the King of the Romans' as the ancestor of Prince Cyngen of Powys. The memory of his legendary wife Helen of the Legions has persisted even longer, for many stretches of Roman road in Wales are still known as 'Sarn Helen' — Elen's Road.

The fort of Segontium — 'Caer Segeint in Arfon' — likewise became a place of proliferating myth, and in another *Mabinogion* tale it is named as the court of Bran the Blessed, a giant king whose head was believed to be buried beneath the Tower of London. *Segontium's* Roman ruins, clearly much more impressive in the early Middle Ages than they are today, doubtless provided inspiration for the 'castle' of the Macsen Wledig story, while the many Roman coins found thereabouts gave rise to the belief that the Emperor Constantine, son of Constantine the Great, had 'sowed three seeds, of gold, of silver and of bronze, in the pavement of that city, so that no man who lived there should ever be poor'. According to Nennius, a Welsh scholar writing in about 800, the tomb of this same Constantine was 'still

Eliseg's Pillar, Llangollen, claims Maximus as an ancestor of the princes of Powys.

pointed out near the city called Caer Segeint, and identified by the letters carved on its stonework'.

Who this Constantine really was is unknown: he cannot have been the historical Emperor Constantine II, who never came to Britain. But the tomb's supposed connection with Constantine the Great (A.D. 306-37), the first Christian emperor of Rome and thus a far more internationally famous figure than Maximus, lent even higher legendary status to the old fort. When the Norman Earl Hugh of Chester built a castle at Caernarfon, indeed, a twelfth-century Welsh writer described it as 'in the old city of the Emperor Constantine, son of Constans the Great'.

Earl Hugh's fortress (like the palace of the native Welsh prices of Gwynedd which succeeded it) was not actually on the site of Roman *Segontium,* but on that of the present Caernarfon Castle, some seven hundred yards (640m) to the west. Yet the legends of an Imperial past, the glamour of Maximus the Prince, Helen of the Legions and Constantine the Great, continued to pervade both the ruined Roman fort and the newer Norman castle. And shortly after King Edward I's arrival at Caernarfon in May 1283, having just completed the conquest of Wales, the ancient tales were triumphantly vindicated by the discovery of a Roman Imperial tomb there.

Top: *A Roman auxiliary soldier. Troops of this type garrisoned the fort of* Segontium *(Illustration by Geraint Derbyshire).*

Middle: *Constantine the Great, a potent figure in the Caernarfon legend (By permission of the Yorkshire Museum).*

Left: *An aerial view of the Roman fort of* Segontium, *with Caernarfon Castle in the distance.*

A feast at King Arthur's Round Table, from a thirteenth-century French manuscript. King Edward I celebrated his Welsh conquests with a tournament called a 'Round Table' at Nefyn (By permission of the British Library, Royal Ms. 14 E III, f.89).

The Legend Vindicated

The news of this discovery caused a sensation in England, and was reported by a number of chroniclers. All of them agreed that the body in the tomb 'was honourably reburied in the nearby church' — presumably St Peblig's, by the Roman fort — 'at the king's own orders'. Some considerable confusion however, seems to have prevailed about whose body had been found. A Westminster chronicler called it 'the corpse of Maximus the Prince, father of the noble Emperor Constantine', but a Worcester monk simply called it 'a mighty prince, father of the Emperor Constantine', while the chronicler at Waverley Abbey in Surrey believed it was no less than 'the body of the great Emperor Constantine' himself.

Seven centuries later, we cannot even guess at the true identity of the body, which may have been found in the tomb mentioned by Nennius about the year 800. It was certainly neither Constantine the Great, who was buried at Constantinople (Istanbul), nor Maximus, who was executed in Yugoslavia — and who was incidentally born at least a generation later than his supposed 'son' Constantine. Indeed, it was almost certainly not a Roman emperor at all. What matters, however, is that King Edward apparently believed he had found confirmation of Caernarfon's Imperial past, with momentous results.

The fourteenth-century Waverley Chronicle records the 'discovery' of Constantine's body at Caernarfon in 1283 (By permission of the British Library, Cotton Ms. Vespasian A XIV, f.191).

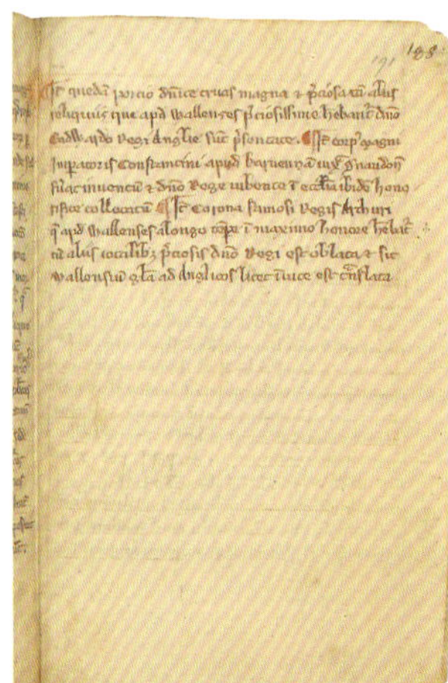

This allegedly Imperial corpse was only one of several fabulous discoveries made during Edward's Welsh campaigns. To the world at large, nothing less could be expected, for thirteenth-century Wales was seen as a land of marvels and mysteries, where one highly imaginative Flemish chronicler claimed that the king had encountered enchanted stags, the rusted armour of giants, and even a magic cave containing the bones of King Arthur. More sober English chroniclers meanwhile recorded a piece of the 'true cross' on which Christ was crucified, presented to the king at Conwy in June 1283, and 'the crown of the once-famous King Arthur', which may have been given to Edward at Caernarfon. Edward treasured the piece of the cross, which he encased in gold and gems and henceforward carried about on his travels, and he was as fascinated as any of his contemporaries by the tales of Arthur. Indeed, he celebrated his Welsh victories with a tournament called a 'Round Table' at Nefyn in the Lleyn peninsula, a place with long Arthurian associations, where a book of Merlin's prophecies had supposedly been found a century before. But what really seized the king's imagination was the Imperial tomb at Caernarfon, where he now began to build one of the greatest of his castles.

The Legends Embodied

There were several good reasons why Edward should have decided to build a castle at Caernarfon. Intended to be the last of his Welsh castles, it closed the stone ring of new or rebuilt fortifications — Conwy, Harlech, Criccieth, Denbigh and the rest — which hemmed in the old Welsh heartland of Snowdonia. As previous conquerors of Wales had discovered, the Caernarfon area was one of great strategic importance, and Edward's new fortress, occupying the site of a Norman castle and a Welsh princely palace, served to emphasize the king's status as both the vanquisher of the Welsh princes and the successor to the Norman monarchs.

None of these factors, however, account for the features which distinguish Caernarfon so markedly from Edward's other Welsh castles, or for that matter from any other medieval fortress in Britain. Nor do they really explain why this ostensibly rather remote stronghold was clearly intended to become the principal English royal palace in conquered Wales. What, then, made Caernarfon so special? The answer seems to be its claims to a magnificent

Imperial past, to which Edward believed himself the legitimate heir by conquest.

At Caernarfon, therefore, Edward set his architect James of St George to design an Imperial castle, a fortress which simultaneously recalled the mighty strongholds of ancient Rome and embodied the dream of the Emperor Maximus. Instead of building the round or semi-circular towers usual in thirteenth-century castles like Conwy or Harlech, Master James therefore laid out Caernarfon's eleven great towers in polygonal form. Such towers had few precedents in medieval England, and their principal inspiration was most probably the polygonal towers on the late Roman walls of Constantinople, the former Byzantium, and Constantine the Great's own city. Edward may also have borne in mind the Roman polygonal ('multangular') tower which still stands at York, the city where Constantine was first proclaimed emperor.

Unlike any other medieval fortress in Britain, moreover, Caernarfon Castle has towers and walls decorated with broad horizontal bands of contrasting coloured masonry. Here again, the inspiration was doubtless the brick-banded walls of Constantinople, reinforced perhaps by the example of the similarly decorated Roman walls at York, or at Richborough, Pevensey, Portchester, and other 'Saxon Shore' Roman forts along the southern English coast.

Apart from echoing Constantine's city, the banded decoration of Caernarfon's walls may also have had another purpose — to recall the 'great towers of various colours' on the castle of Macsen Wledig's dream. A similar motive surely prompted the three carved eagles which originally surmounted the triple turrets of the Eagle Tower, the largest and most important of Caernarfon's towers. Eagles, of course, were the symbols of Imperial Rome, and tradition holds that one of those on the Eagle Tower was actually Roman, and brought from *Segontium*. But they also appeared in Macsen's vision, carved upon the throne of the dream-maiden's father.

A king and his master mason, by Matthew Paris about 1250. At Caernarfon King Edward I set his architect to design no less than an Imperial stronghold (By permission of the British Library, Cotton Ms. Nero D I, f.23v).

For all its undoubted military strength, then, Caernarfon Castle is above all an embodiment of legend, and a graphic demonstration of the power that legend had even over the otherwise hard-headed Edward I. Viewing the castle from across the River Seiont, with the many-towered town walls marching away to the north, it is still easy to imagine it as the fortress of Macsen Wledig's dream — 'a great city at the mouth of the river, and in the city a great castle . . . with many great towers of various colours on the castle'. Almost as soon as building work on the castle had begun, moreover, the birth there of a royal prince opened a new chapter in the legend of Caernarfon.

The mighty fifth-century walls of Roman Constantinople, with their polygonal towers and brick-banded decoration. They may have provided the inspiration for the style and decoration at Caernarfon.

Princes in Wales, Princes of Wales

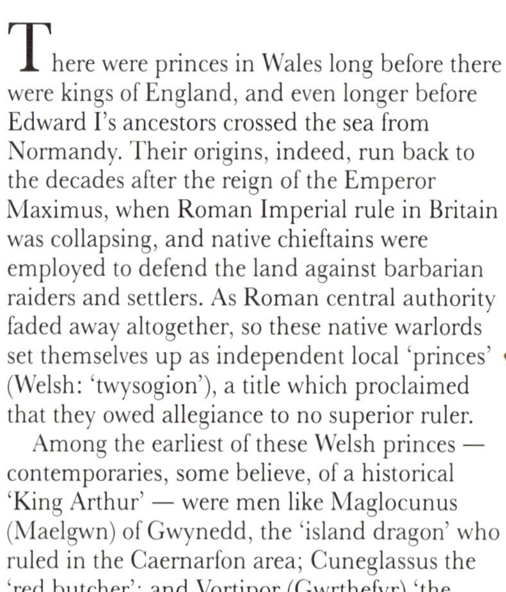

The eleventh-century Carew cross commemorates Maredudd ap Edwin (d. 1035), prince of the pre-Conquest kingdom of Deheubarth (south-west Wales).

There were princes in Wales long before there were kings of England, and even longer before Edward I's ancestors crossed the sea from Normandy. Their origins, indeed, run back to the decades after the reign of the Emperor Maximus, when Roman Imperial rule in Britain was collapsing, and native chieftains were employed to defend the land against barbarian raiders and settlers. As Roman central authority faded away altogether, so these native warlords set themselves up as independent local 'princes' (Welsh: 'twysogion'), a title which proclaimed that they owed allegiance to no superior ruler.

Among the earliest of these Welsh princes — contemporaries, some believe, of a historical 'King Arthur' — were men like Maglocunus (Maelgwn) of Gwynedd, the 'island dragon' who ruled in the Caernarfon area; Cuneglassus the 'red butcher'; and Vortipor (Gwrthefyr) 'the tyrant of the Demetae', whose tombstone stood in Castelldwyran churchyard near Carmarthen. The sixth-century monk Gildas, who yearned for the old Roman order, condemned them roundly in Latin. But as the memory of Rome faded, household bards praised their successors in Welsh, hymning their battles against Irish raiders and encroaching Saxons, and later against Vikings and Normans, but most of all against rival Welsh princes.

The memorial of Prince Vortipor (Gwyrthefyr), described by the monk Gildas in the sixth century as 'the tyrant of the Demetae'. The stone lay in the churchyard at Castelldwyran near Carmarthen (By courtesy of the National Monuments Record, Wales).

A Welsh prince as lawgiver, from a mid thirteenth-century copy of the great Welsh law book of Hywel Dda — Hywel the Good, d. 949/50 (By courtesy of the National Library of Wales, Peniarth Ms. 28, f.1v).

For though these heroic figures were princes *in* Wales, they were in no sense princes *of* Wales, ruling a united Welsh nation; until a decade or so before Edward I's conquest, indeed, there was no united nation to rule. Instead, Wales was a chequerboard of independent princely states — the most important being Gwynedd in the north-west, Dyfed in the south-west, Powys in the east, and Morgannwg, Brycheiniog and Gwent in the south-east — whose boundaries and allegiance fluctuated with the tides of dynastic warfare. According to the twelfth-century observer Gerald of Wales (himself of part-Norman, part-Welsh ancestry) it was this endemic lack of unity which prevented the Welsh from decisively repulsing their enemies: 'they will not', he wrote, 'subject themselves to the authority of one ruler, like other nations . . . if only they had one prince, and he a good one, I cannot see how so powerful a people could ever be completely conquered'.

During the centuries which divided the Romans from the Normans, admittedly, individual princes had from time to time won a temporary and personal ascendancy over their rivals. Nearly all such 'over-princes' sprang from the royal line of Gwynedd, which claimed descent from the Virgin Mary's cousin and — rather more credibly — from Cunedda Wledig, who drove the Irish invaders from north-west Wales in the fifth century. His successors included Cadwallon, 'King of the Britons' (d. 634), who campaigned as far afield as Hadrian's Wall; Rhodri Fawr (d. 877), who

The 'tombstone' of Catamanus (Cadfan), 'the wisest and most renowned of all kings', who ruled Gwynedd in the early seventh century. The stone is at the church of Llangadwaladr, Anglesey (By courtesy of the National Monuments Record, Wales).

Above: *The arms traditionally attributed to Owain Gwynedd (d. 1170), who may well have signalled his pre-eminence in Wales by adopting the title 'prince of the Welsh'.*

Below: *The privy seal of Prince Llywelyn the Great, who came to dominate almost the whole of Wales by 1215 (By permission of the National Museum of Wales).*

repulsed the Vikings and united most of Wales; and Rhodri's grandson Hywel Dda (d. 949/50), the so-called law giver, who minted perhaps the only native Welsh coinage.

Though the unifying influence of these rulers did not outlast their deaths, during the twelfth and thirteenth centuries the prestige of the Gwyneddian princes steadily increased, mainly due to their success in defending their territory against the Norman 'Marchers' who had swallowed up much of south and east Wales. By 1115 the princes had recovered Caernarfon, which henceforward became a Welsh royal residence, and under Owain Gwynedd (1137-70) they temporarily extended their borders almost to Chester. Owain's grandson Llywelyn the Great (1201-40) consolidated his victories, and by an adroit combination of diplomacy and warfare came to dominate almost the whole of Wales by 1215.

Not until 1258, however, did Llywelyn's grandson Llywelyn ap Gruffudd adopt the title of 'prince of Wales', making Gwynedd the focus of a united Welsh state. To do so he had not only to overcome the resentment of lesser Welsh rulers, but also to gain the acceptance of his potentially much more formidable English neighbours, then weakened by civil strife between Henry III and his barons. By intervening in these wars, Llywelyn finally gained English recognition of his title in 1267. The state thus established — the independent 'principality of Wales' — covered rather more than half the country, though it still excluded the southern and eastern lands of the Anglo-Norman 'Marchers'. Doubtless Llywelyn hoped to annex these in time, but within a decade his ambitions clashed head-on with those of the vengeful Edward I, king of a once-again united England. The war of 1277 pushed Llywelyn back into Gwynedd, and an attempted counter-stroke five years later ended in utter disaster: on 11 December 1282 Llywelyn fell in a skirmish at Cilmeri near Builth, speared by an English soldier who had no idea who his victim was. So died Llywelyn ap Gruffudd, called in Welsh 'Y Llyw Olaf', 'the Last Prince'. He was indeed the first, last, and only Welsh prince of an independent Wales, but his principality did not die with him. Taken over first by Edward I and subsequently by Edward of Caernarfon and his English successors, it would endure as an institution for another two and a half centuries, until King Henry VIII united principality and marcher lands to form the Wales we know today. In many ways, therefore, Llywelyn was as much 'the first' as 'the last' prince of Wales.

Right: *'Llywelyn Prince of Wales': the first, last and only Welsh prince of an independent Wales. This imaginative portrait comes from a sixteenth-century manuscript (By gracious permission of Her Majesty the Queen, Royal Library, Wriothesley Ms. quire B).*

The First English Prince of Wales

The Birth of a Prince

Edward, son of King Edward I and his Queen Eleanor of Castile, was born at Caernarfon on 25 April 1284: and a few days later, the royal baby was proclaimed there as the first English prince of Wales. The first of these statements is undoubted fact, but the second — though hallowed by centuries of retelling — needs rather more careful consideration. Here is the usual version of the proclamation story, couched in the early Victorian prose of Mrs Strickland, authoress of *The Lives of the Queens of England* (1840):

'The king hastened directly to Caernarvon to see his Eleanora and her boy: and three days after, the castle was the rendezvous of all the chiefs of North Wales, who met to tender their final submission to Edward I, and to implore him, as their lord paramount, to appoint them a prince who was a native of their own country, and whose native tongue was neither French nor Saxon, which they assured him they could not understand'.

'Edward told them he would immediately appoint them a prince who could speak neither English nor French. The Welsh magnates, expecting he was a kinsman of their royal line, declared they would instantly accept him as their prince, if his character was void of reproach: whereupon the king ordered his infant son to be brought in and presented to them, assuring the assembly that he was just born a native of their country, that he could not speak a word of English or French, and, if they pleased, the first words he uttered should be in Welsh'.

'The fierce mountaineers little expected such a ruler; they had, however, no alternative but submission, and, with as good a grace as they might, kissed the tiny hand which was to sway their sceptre, and vowed fealty to the babe of the faithful Eleanora'.

This pretty tale, however, has provoked much doubt among historians. They do not dispute that young Edward was eventually declared the first English prince of Wales, but point out that his formal appointment did not occur until he was sixteen years old, and that it actually took place at Lincoln in 1301. No contemporary record calls him prince of Wales before that date. At the time of Edward's birth, moreover, he was not the heir to the throne. For his eleven year old elder brother, Alfonso, was then still alive, and if anyone was likely to have been declared prince of Wales in 1284, it was Alfonso — who was certainly not so created. No mention of any proclamation ceremony in Wales, in fact, can be traced to a date before 1584 — exactly three centuries after the supposed event — when the Welsh clergyman Dr David Powel set down the story in these words (spelling modernized):

Left: *Baby Edward of Caernarfon proclaimed Prince of Wales. A Victorian reconstruction of an event which probably never occurred (By courtesy of Gwynedd County Council).*

'King Edward, albeit he had brought all Wales under his subjection . . . yet he could never win the common people of the country to accept him for their prince . . . Neither could he bring them to yield their obedience to any other prince, except he were of their own nation. For the Welshmen could not abide to have any Englishman to be their ruler, (but) oftentimes upon the king's motion answered, that they were content to take for their prince any man whom his majesty would name, so that he were a Welshman: and none other answer could he ever get of them by any means'.

'Whereupon the king sent for Queen Eleanor out of England in the deep of winter, being then great with child, to the castle of Caernarfon. And when she was nigh to be brought to bed, the king went to Rhuddlan, and sent for all the barons and best men in all Wales to come to him. And when they were come, he deferred the consultation, until he was certified that the queen was delivered of a son: then . . . he called the Welshmen together, declaring unto them, that whereas they were oftentimes suitors unto him to appoint them a prince . . . he would name them a prince, if they would allow and obey him whom he should name. To which motion they answered that they would so do, if he would appoint one of their own nation to be their prince. Whereunto the king replied, that he would name one that was born in Wales, and could speak never a word of English, whose life and conversation no man was able to stain. And when they all had granted that such a one they would obey, he named his own son Edward, born in Caernarfon castle a few days before'.

Above: *The seal of Edward II [cast] as prince of Wales (By permission of the National Museum of Wales).*

Below: *The title page of Dr David Powel's* Historie of Cambria *(1584).*

Right: *Dr Powel's volume includes the earliest known version of the proclamation tale (By permission of the National Museum of Wales).*

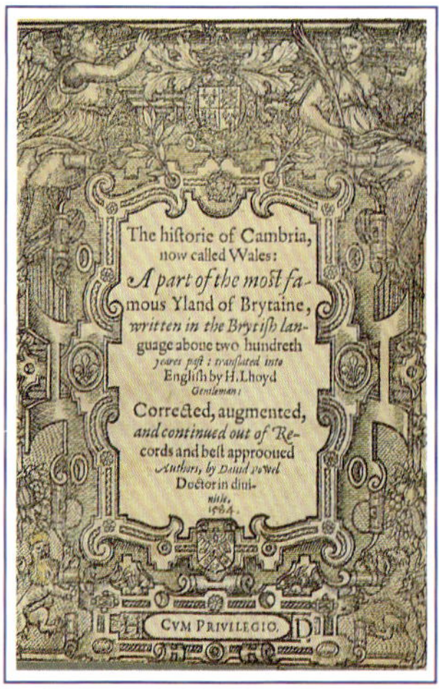

The historie of Cambria, now called Wales:
A part of the most famous Yland of Brytaine, written in the Brytish language aboue two hundreth yeares past: translated into English by H. Lhoyd *Gentleman:*
Corrected, augmented, *and continued out of Records and best approoued Authors, by David Powel* Doctor in diuinitie. 1584.
CVM PRIVILEGIO.

Dr Powel's original version of the story thus differs markedly from the later and better-known variants: for its action takes place, not at Caernarfon, but at Rhuddlan Castle, some forty miles (64km) to the east. Nor are either the baby Edward or Queen Eleanor actually present at the 'proclamation' of the prince. These very factors give Powel's tale some ring of truth. For other sources also suggest that the king was at Rhuddlan both before and after the time of young Edward's birth, and Rhuddlan Castle, almost completed in 1284, would certainly have been a far more convenient setting for an assembly of Welsh notables than the building site that was then the scarcely-begun castle at Caernarfon. Powel's version, moreover, does not make the 'proclamation' of the prince of Wales anything like as formal an occasion as was later envisaged. It is more in the nature of a rather poor joke, of the kind that King Edward is known to have loved.

Where Dr Powel got his story from is quite unknown: but he was himself a native of north Wales, where he could well have picked up a genuine oral tradition, handed down by word of mouth from generation to generation. And if the king really did jest about making a speechless infant 'prince of Wales' in 1284, he may well have remembered the jest sixteen years later, when the baby had grown into a teenage prince, an heir to the throne who needed lands of his own to support him during his father's lifetime.

76 The Princes of VVales

The Princes of VVales of the blood *royall of England : collected for the* most part out of the Records *in the Towre.*

Edward of Caernaruon.

King Edward, albeit hee had brought al Wales vnder his ſubiection : and by a ſtatute made at Ruthlan, An. 12. Ed. 1. incorporated and vnited the ſame vnto England: in the which ſtatute there be many good lawes concerning the diuiſion of Wales into counties, and concerning diuerſe offices and officers, and concerning triall, and concerning the diuiſions of actions, and the forme of manie writs, and the proceeding therein, much like to the lawes of England: yet he could neuer winne the good will of the common people of the countrie to accept him for their Prince, and to be obedient vnto ſuch officers as he ſhould appoint to gouerne them, vnleſſe he would remaine himſelfe in the countrie among them. Neither could he bring them to yeeld their obedience to anie other Prince, except he were of their owne nation: for the Welſhmen hauing experience of the gouernment of the Engliſh officers, and knowing that the king would rule the countrie by his deputies, cold not abide to haue anie Engliſhman to be their ruler: who oftentimes vpon the kings motion anſwered, that they were content to take for their Prince anie man, whom his Maieſtie would

One aspect of Powel's story, at any rate, can be corroborated with some certainty: namely that young Edward's birth at Caernarfon was a matter of deliberate policy. It seems likely that the king wished his son to be born in the legendary city of Maximus and Constantine, and it is certainly difficult to see why else the heavily pregnant Queen Eleanor should have been brought to a castle which in 1284 consisted of little more than a ditch and a stockade, some temporary timber apartments, and perhaps a half-completed tower.

Queen Eleanor, of course, was well used to accompanying her restless husband on his travels. Ever since their marriage thirty years before — when he was fifteen and she perhaps two or three years younger — she had followed him devotedly all over his dominions, which stretched from the Scottish border to the Pyrenees. She had even joined him on Crusade, witnessing an attempt on his life by a Muslim assassin with a poisoned dagger, and is said to have wept so noisily that she had to be dragged from the room while the poison was cut out. Nor, at the age of about 42, was the Spanish-born queen any stranger to pregnancy. Young Edward would be at least her fourteenth (and last) child, though by the time of his birth only six of her previous children — her son Alfonso and five daughters — were still living.

Edward I (left) from a manuscript illustration of 1297 in which he is depicted confronting his then bitter enemy King Philip IV of France (Copyright: Public Record Office, E 368/69, m.54).

Queen Eleanor of Castile (d. 1290), wife of Edward I and mother of the first English prince of Wales, from her splendid tomb-effigy in Westminster Abbey (By courtesy of the Warburg Institute).

All the same, Eleanor took six days to cover the forty or so miles (64km) from the comparative comfort of Rhuddlan Castle, arriving at Caernarfon on 1 April. No doubt she travelled in her cushion-padded coach, while her state robes followed aboard a pair of packhorses in the care of 'little Robin the tailor', who had brought them all the way from London. They would be worn at the Easter festivities held at Caernarfon on 9 April, whereafter the queen settled down to await her baby, doubtless fortified by the grateful prayers of the many 'poor and infirm folk' whom the royal family had recently assisted. Eighty yards (73m) of cloth and 114 pairs of shoes had been distributed to them on Maundy Thursday (6 April), and in the weeks before the birth thirteen paupers were fed at the then quite adequate cost of 1d. (3p) a day each, 'by the king's order, because the queen was pregnant'.

The child was born on 25 April. This is the feast of St Mark, and in medieval times it was sometimes regarded as a day of ill-omen, when black-veiled crosses were carried in penitential procession to ward off ill-health and ill-fortune in the coming year. But at Caernarfon it was a day of rejoicing — perhaps especially for the 200 paupers who were fed in honour of the saint, and the hundreds more who got an extra treat to celebrate the prince's birth. Edward would continue to mark his birthday in the same liberal manner throughout much of his life, feeding as many hundred paupers as the year of life he had attained: on 25 April 1300, therefore, he provided meals for no less than 1,700 of them.

Exactly where in Caernarfon Edward was born is unknown. Tradition points out as his birthplace a small and comfortless room on the first floor of the Eagle Tower, only about 12 feet long by 8 feet broad (3.7m by 2.4m), and lacking a fireplace. But though the Eagle Tower was among the first stone buildings in the castle to be raised, it may not have been completed even to first-floor height by April 1284. If it had, even the hard-bitten Eleanor would surely have preferred to give birth in the principal central chamber of the tower's first floor, rather than in the 'little dark den' of tradition. Indeed, she may well have chosen to avoid the masons and the debris of construction altogether, and to take up residence either in the town or else in the timber buildings which had been erected in the castle courtyard during the previous year.

These timber buildings were no mere sheds. They included eight 'chambers', including one for the king and queen; their walls were plastered, and they even boasted 'a lawn for the queen', laid down in turf by 'Hamo of the Queen's Chamber'. Indeed, Eleanor loved gardens, and later on imported experts from her native Spain to improve her English flower-beds. Not long before the birth, moreover, Simon the Glazier of Chester had made nine new windows in the royal chamber within the timber buildings. So it seems quite likely that it was in this chamber, and through these windows, that baby 'Edward of Caernarfon' first saw the light of day.

Heavy with child, Queen Eleanor travelled from Rhuddlan to Caernarfon in late March, 1284. The journey was no doubt made in her cushion-padded coach, similar perhaps to this travelling coach for royal ladies depicted in the mid fourteenth-century Luttrell Psalter (By permission of the British Library, Additional Ms. 42130, f.181).

Edward of Caernarfon was born on 25 April 1284. Precisely where amid the debris of construction at the castle Queen Eleanor chose to give birth we cannot be certain. This late fifteenth-century manuscript illustration gives some impression of such a royal event (By permission of the British Library, Cotton Ms. Julius E IV, Art.6, f.22v).

A Lonely Childhood: 1284-1301

If Dr Powel's story is to be believed, the baby's royal father was away from Caernarfon at the time of his birth. According to tradition, the news was brought to the king at Rhuddlan by a Welshman named Gruffudd Llwyd, who was rewarded for his errand by the gift of the manor of Dinorwig near Llanberis (Certainly this same Gruffudd, a distant ancestor of the Tudor royal family, became in later years young Edward's chief Welsh supporter). But it is harder to credit Powel's statement that King Edward did not even attend the child's christening at Caernarfon on 1 May, especially in view of the fact that the boy was named after him. On the other hand, it must be admitted that neither King Edward nor Queen Eleanor were particularly attentive parents, even by medieval standards.

The chamber on the first floor of the Eagle Tower, traditionally the birthplace of Edward of Caernarfon.

Even the most doting royal mother, however, was not expected to nourish her child with her own milk. Soon after the birth, therefore, baby Edward was handed over to a 'wet nurse' named Mary or 'Marrola' Maunsel, reputedly a Welshwoman and certainly a resident of Caernarfon — where she was later to enjoy a comfortable old age on a handsome royal pension. Under her care, Edward remained in or near Caernarfon for the first four months or so of his life: it is perhaps unlikely that he accompanied his parents on their thanksgiving pilgrimage to holy Bardsey Island — where 20,000 saints were reputedly buried — or to the 'Round Table' tournament at Nefyn — a glittering occasion marred only by the sudden collapse of a dance hall, 'where many noblemen were shamelessly revelling'.

Baby Edward was christened at Caernarfon on 1 May 1284. As this later medieval manuscript illustration shows, such ceremonies were important events. It would be surprising if King Edward did not attend (By permission of the British Library, Cotton Ms. Julius E IV, Art.6, f.1v).

As the summer of 1284 drew to a close, Edward and two of his sisters set out from Caernarfon towards England. He was not to return to Wales for another sixteen years, and in fact never visited Caernarfon again. On the way, at Rhuddlan, nurse Marrola fell ill, and was replaced by an Englishwoman called Alice Leygrave, later significantly described as the 'king's mother . . . who suckled him in his youth'.

Though by now heir to the throne — his elder brother Alfonso having died in August 1284 — Edward saw comparatively little of his real parents during his childhood. His mother died in 1290, and his grandmother Eleanor of Provence, (who had fussed and clucked over him in a manner still observable among grandparents), in 1291. King Edward, now growing increasingly grim and cantankerous with age, had little time to spare for him, and his chief boyhood companion seems to have been his sister Elizabeth, known as 'the Welshwoman' because of her birth at Rhuddlan in 1282. Like all medieval royal personages, moreover, much of young Edward's life was spent on the move. His only real home was the manor of King's Langley in Hertfordshire, where he passed the winter months before setting off again on his summer travels: during the summer of 1293, for instance, the nine year old prince visited no less than 64 places, rarely spending more than two nights in any of them.

Lonely though it apparently was, Edward's boyhood was not of course entirely devoid of pleasure. He can be glimpsed playing with a toy castle given to him by his father, or enjoying the antics of a certain female acrobat called 'Matilda Makejoy', who 'made her vaults' for the thirteen year old Edward at Christmas 1296. Nor was he entirely cut off from Welsh influences. In 1290, for instance, a man from Caernarfon brought him a present of four herons, and in 1300 he was sent a pair of Welsh greyhounds from Conwy, while a number of Welshmen were permanently employed in his household. Some of these were probably the amateur or professional minstrels who laid the foundations of Edward's well-attested love for the 'crwth' or 'crowd', a kind of bowed lyre which rivalled the harp as the national instrument of medieval Wales.

The First Prince of Wales: 1301-07

Edward's formal connection with the land of his birth, however, began only on 7 February 1301, when he was officially created prince of Wales and earl of Chester — titles borne by most heirs to the throne ever since. The honour was granted during a parliament held at Lincoln, and though no record survives of any investiture ceremony, such a ceremony did very probably take place, perhaps in Lincoln Cathedral's magnificent new chapter house. For when the next prince of Wales ('The Black Prince') was created four decades later, reference was made to a 'custom' — which can only mean one established in 1301 — of investiture 'by the placing of a coronet on the head, a ring on the finger, and a silver rod in the hand'. The coronet used may well have been the golden 'talaith' ('diadem') which had belonged to Prince Llywelyn ap Gruffudd, the last native ruler of north Wales, and which was carried off to Westminster Abbey after the elder Edward's conquests.

The title was no empty honour, for it gave Edward control of all the royal lands and castles in Wales, whose considerable revenues he would henceforth receive. Before he could do so, however, he had to take physical 'homage' from his new subjects. So in the spring of 1301 he spent five weeks at the north Welsh castles of

Lincoln Cathedral, perhaps the scene of Edward's Investiture as prince of Wales in 1301.

Edward of Caernarfon created prince of Wales, by King Edward I. The honour was granted during a parliament held at Lincoln in February 1301 (By permission of the British Library, Cotton Ms. Nero D II, f.191v).

Above: *A thirteenth-century Welsh archer. Many hundreds of the famous Welsh archers served with Edward in his Scottish wars (From the* Littere Wallie *— Copyright: Public Record Office, E36/274).*

Right: *Conwy Castle, where Edward received the homage of Welsh landowners in the spring of 1301.*

One chronicler said of the banquet which followed Edward's formal knighting that nothing so splendid had been seen since King Arthur was crowned at Caerleon. This early fourteenth-century manuscript illustration shows musicians entertaining at a banquet (By permission of the British Library, Additional Ms. 28162, f.10v).

A Welsh 'crwth' or bowed lyre, Edward's favourite instrument (By permission of the National Museum of Wales, Welsh Folk Museum).

Flint, Hope, Ruthin, Rhuddlan and Conwy, where perhaps a thousand Welsh landowners came to kneel individually before him, placing their hands in his while repeating their oaths of loyalty. On one day alone he dealt with 170 such ceremonies, so it is perhaps not surprising that he allowed himself a day off on his birthday.

Edward was not to visit Wales again as prince, but English chroniclers believed he had made a deep impression on its people; 'who esteemed him their rightful lord, because he derived his origin from those parts'. Certainly many hundreds of the famous Welsh archers served under him in the Scottish wars which were henceforward to occupy much of his time — and during which he was also accompanied by a symbolic pet lion, complete with its own travelling cart. His undoubted enthusiasm for Welsh music, moreover, attracted many Welsh minstrels to the most magnificent occasion of his time as prince, his formal knighting at Westminster on Whit Sunday 1306.

Some three hundred other young men, attracted by King Edward's offer of free armour, robes and ceremonial bed to all suitable candidates, were knighted with him: and accounts of the resulting pandemonium present a startling contrast with the restrained dignity of modern royal occasions. On the night before the ceremony, when Edward and his fellow candidates were supposed to be keeping solemn vigil in Westminster Abbey, the noise of trumpets and shouting outside was so loud that the monks' chants could not be heard from one side of the church to the other. On the day itself the disorder in the abbey was so great that two knights were crushed to death, while several more fainted. Fortunately, the prince himself had already been knighted privately an hour or so beforehand, but warhorses had to be used to clear him enough space to confer a similar honour on his companions.

The banquet that followed was better organized, and one chronicler believed that nothing so splendid had been seen since King Arthur was crowned at Caerleon. Its climax was the entrance of a pair of swans accompanied by 80 minstrels, including David, Tegwaret and Owen, the Welsh crwth players, and 'Good Hugh', the Welsh harper. On these swans (whether they were alive, cooked or artificial is not at all clear) the prince swore never to rest until he and his father had defeated Robert the Bruce and conquered Scotland.

His vow was never to be fulfilled. Edward was already on bad terms with his father, who disapproved of the 'excessive' affection he lavished on a young Gascon knight called Piers Gaveston. The quarrel came to a head when he asked the king's permission to give Gaveston some of his own lands. The old man became so furious that he tore out handfuls of Edward's long hair, kicked him to the floor, and then banished Gaveston from the realm. So the old king's death, still on campaign, probably caused his son little sorrow. On the day it occurred, 7 July 1307, the first prince of Wales became King Edward II of England.

In this manuscript illustration a prince receives the sword of knighthood. Prince Edward was knighted at Westminster Abbey on Whit Sunday 1306. Many Welsh minstrels were present at this magnificent occasion (By permission of the British Library, Royal Ms.20 D IX, f.134v).

Above: *The statue of Edward of Caernarfon (King Edward II) above the King's Gate at Caernarfon Castle.*

Left: *The Eagle Tower at Caernarfon, traditionally (though by no means certainly) the birthplace of Prince Edward. Each of the three turrets which surmount the tower was to bear a stone eagle — a symbol of an Imperial past, to which King Edward I believed himself a legitimate heir by conquest* *(see p. 9)*.

The Welshmen's King: 1307-27

Edward was not a successful monarch. For though his English subjects at first admired his tall, handsome appearance and excellent horsemanship, they soon came to disapprove most strongly of many of his other activities. Chroniclers sneered at his interest in 'rustic arts' like ditching and thatching, and his enthusiasm for swimming and rowing, which they thought no fit occupations for a gentleman, still less for a king. They were also suspicious of his liking for plays and the company of actors and crwth players, and believed that Walter Reynolds, whom he made archbishop of Canterbury, had gained royal favour largely by his expertise as a producer of court pageants.

More seriously, both chroniclers and English barons were horrified by the extravagant favours Edward showered on the flamboyant Piers Gaveston, and later the grasping Hugh le Despenser. But even this might have been forgiven him, had he not proved so spectacularly unsuccessful in his wars against Robert the Bruce and the Scots. The disaster of Bannockburn (1314), and the Scottish raids which followed — on one occasion chasing Edward all over Yorkshire — were a stinging and unforgivable blow to English martial pride.

Throughout all these upheavals, however, many of his Welsh subjects remained loyal to 'Edward of Caernarfon', perhaps partly because they preferred his rule to the exactions of the rapacious English 'Marcher' barons of south Wales and the borders. When civil war broke out between Edward and his English opponents in 1321, the Welsh took his side with enthusiasm: led by Sir Gruffudd Llwyd — the man who is said to have brought the news of his birth to his father — they contributed significantly to his eventual victory. It was at about this time, incidentally, that Edward's statue was erected above the King's Gate at Caernarfon Castle, where its weather-worn remains still stand. Its royal dignity, however, is no longer maintained by the original 'twelve iron spikes, to protect the head of the king's statue, so that birds do not sit upon it'.

Edward's Welsh-assisted triumph of 1322 proved only temporary. When the next crisis came in 1326, it was in south Wales that he sought refuge from his now all-conquering opponents, led by his own wife Queen Isabella and her lover, the Marcher lord Roger Mortimer, of Wigmore Castle in Herefordshire. But Sir Gruffudd Llwyd, besieged by Mortimer's forces somewhere in north Wales, was powerless to help him, and in October 1326 he was betrayed into the hands of his pursuers near Llantrisant.

King Edward II, 'The Welshmen's King', from his tomb-effigy in Gloucester Cathedral — the Benedictine abbey of St Peter at the time of his burial (By courtesy of the Conway Library, Courtauld Institute of Art).

Welshmen — and a constable of Caernarfon Castle — likewise played a crucial role in the final act of Edward's tragedy. After his deposition and imprisonment at Berkeley Castle in Gloucestershire, a band of Welsh loyalists led by Sir Rhys ap Gruffudd hatched a desperate plot to cross the Severn and rescue him. Rumours of the conspiracy, however, reached William Shalford, an English townsman of Caernarfon who was then serving as constable of the castle. Shalford was also one of Mortimer's agents, so he passed the information straight to his master, warning that a 'suitable remedy' was needed to prevent Edward's rescue and Mortimer's consequent overthrow. According to some contemporaries at least, it was this letter which prompted Mortimer to arrange a 'suitable remedy' indeed: a fortnight after it was written, on 21 October 1327, Edward of Caernarfon was brutally murdered in Berkeley Castle. 'For long afterwards', wrote a wondering English chronicler, 'the Welshmen sang sad songs about him in their own language, for they loved him in death as they had in life'.

The Princes and Princesses of Wales

The seal of the Black Prince as prince of Wales. It includes the earliest known depiction of the famous ostrich plume badge of the English princes (By permission of the British Library, Additional Charter, 11308).

The Black Prince

Edward, second Prince of Wales 1343-76

Unlike his unorthodox grandfather the first prince, 'the Black Prince' was the ideal knightly hero. Tall and strong, he was a brave and highly successful soldier, sincerely pious, generous to his followers, and conventional in everything except his surprising marriage to Joan of Kent.

Edward was born at Woodstock in Oxfordshire in 1330, the eldest son of King Edward III and Queen Philippa of Hainault. As a child he kept pet white hares, but his military training began early, and he was given his first suits of armour at the age of eight. Four years later, in May 1343, he was invested as prince of Wales at Westminster, 'with coronet, ring, and silver rod'. Though he never actually visited his principality, he used it as a fertile recruiting ground for his many campaigns in Europe. His Welsh archers and spearmen (enlisted on pain of imprisonment) wore parti-coloured coats and hats of green and white cloth, which may either have echoed or inspired the green and white colours of the Welsh flag.

These archers played a major part in his battles, which began in 1346 when his father invaded France. Knighted as the army landed, the sixteen year old prince commanded a division at the famous victory of Creçy, where he bore the brunt of the fighting and 'won his spurs'. There he killed blind King John of Bohemia, a noted warrior who sported an ostrich plume in his helmet: according to some contemporaries, this was the origin of the ostrich feather badge adopted by Prince Edward, and used by all successive princes of Wales ever since. He bore it on a black shield and pennon, which may have prompted his nickname — not recorded until early Tudor times — of 'the Black Prince'. Others believed, however, that he derived the ostrich plume from a device of his mother's family, and his two mottoes, 'Ich dien' ('I serve') and 'Houmout' ('Pride') were

A knightly hero: the Black Prince, from his magnificent gilt-bronze tomb-effigy in the Trinity Chapel, Canterbury Catherdral. The prince requested in his will that the effigy show a knight 'armed in steel for battle with our arms quartered; and my visage with our helmet of the leopard put under the head of the image'.

In this near-contemporary manuscript illustration, the Black Prince does homage to his father King Edward III (By permission of the British Library, Cotton Ms. Nero D VI, f.32).

certainly couched in the German dialect of her homeland. The first of these mottoes is likewise still used by the princes of Wales.

Certainly, too, 'service' and 'pride' continued to be the ruling maxims of Edward's career. In 1356 he led his Anglo-Welsh army to a hard-fought but decisive victory at Poitiers, where he captured King John of France, and in 1367 and 1369 he gained further victories at Najera in Spain and Limoges in south-western France. By then, however, Edward was becoming a sick man, apparently plagued by recurrent bouts of amoebic dysentery. Forced into unwilling retirement, he died in 1376 on Trinity Sunday (8 June), a feast he had always celebrated with special devotion. He was buried in a magnificent tomb which is still to be seen in the Trinity Chapel of Canterbury Cathedral, where his original regalia for war and tournament are likewise still displayed. A year later his father Edward III followed him to the grave, and his son Richard II acceded to the throne.

The Fair Maid of Kent

Joan, Princess of Wales 1361-85, wife of the Black Prince

'In her time the most beautiful woman in England, and the most amorous': thus a contemporary described Joan of Kent, the first and most romantic medieval princess of Wales. She was born in 1328, the daughter of Thomas, earl of Kent, and granddaughter of Edward I. Brought up at court, at the age of fifteen or sixteen she privately married the one-eyed soldier Sir Thomas Holland: but their marriage was kept secret, and shortly afterwards her unknowing guardians married her to the earl of Salisbury, while Holland was away campaigning. On his return, however, he resolved to recover his rightful wife, and successfully petitioned the Pope for the annulment of her second 'marriage'. Thereafter she returned to Sir Thomas, bearing him three sons and two daughters.

Princess Joan, depicted in a manuscript from St Alban's Abbey, of which both she and Prince Edward were benefactors (By permission of the British Library, Cotton Ms. Nero D VII, f.17v).

Holland died in 1360, leaving Joan — by medieval standards — a middle-aged widow of thirty-three. Within six months, however, she was betrothed to her slightly younger cousin the Black Prince, and in October 1361 they were married. Their wedding provoked much surprise in England, for as heir to the throne Edward was expected to make a political marriage to a young foreign princess. One Welsh border chronicler sneeringly quoted her ironical nickname 'the virgin of Kent' (later changed to the politer 'Fair Maid of Kent'), while French gossips insinuated that she had entrapped Edward by underhand means. But in fact the marriage was clearly a love match — something almost unknown among medieval royalty — and may well have been founded on long-standing attraction, for the pair had known each other as children.

Joan bore her new husband two sons, of whom the survivor became Richard II. After the Black Prince's death, she therefore continued to enjoy high status as the king's mother, playing a prominent part in the troubled opening events of his reign. During the Peasants' Revolt of 1381, for instance, she is said to have escaped from a band of rebels only by allowing them to kiss her. But this admirable and courageous lady chiefly gained respect as a reconciler of family and political quarrels, and in 1385 (though 'now so fat from over-eating that she could scarcely drag herself about') she spared no effort to make peace between Richard and his uncle John of Gaunt. Later in the same year, however, she failed to reconcile the king with Sir John Holland (her son by her first marriage) and consequently died of grief.

Richard of Bordeaux

Richard, third Prince of Wales 1376-77, afterwards King Richard II 1377-99

Born in Bordeaux in January 1367, Richard was the second but only surviving son of the Black Prince and Princess Joan. He was prince of Wales for just seven months, between his creation in November 1376 and the death of his grandfather Edward III in June 1377, whereupon the ten year old boy succeeded as Richard II. As king he visited Wales several times, and like his great-grandfather, Edward of Caernarfon, enjoyed considerable support there, employing Welsh archers in his personal bodyguard.

Like Edward, too, he ended his unhappy and turbulent reign in Wales. When his cousin Henry Bolingbroke invaded England in 1399, Richard was in Ireland: hurrying back, he landed in Pembrokeshire and marched northward to take temporary refuge in Caernarfon Castle, 'where he had nothing to lie down upon but straw, for truly not a farthing's worth of victuals could be found'. Then he moved on to Conwy, but was tricked into leaving its strong walls and ambushed near Rhuddlan by Bolingbroke's supporters. Despite Welsh efforts to rescue him, he was taken to London, deposed and eventually murdered on the orders of Bolingbroke, who succeeded him as Henry IV.

Richard, third prince of Wales, as King Richard II, from a contemporary portrait in Westminster Abbey.

Harry Monmouth

Henry, fourth Prince of Wales 1399-1413, afterwards King Henry V 1413-22

Excepting Edward of Caernarfon, Henry was the only English prince of Wales born in his principality, and the only one who had to fight for his title. He was born in Monmouth Castle in September 1387, the eldest surviving son of Henry Bolingbroke, earl of Derby, and Mary Bohun, heiress of an old Welsh border baronial family. At the time of his birth, his father was merely the first cousin of the reigning King Richard II, who made young Henry his favourite godson and knighted him at the age of eleven.

In 1399, however, Bolingbroke deposed Richard and seized power as King Henry IV: young Henry is said to have parted from his displaced royal godfather in tears. Now heir to the throne, the twelve year old boy was created prince of Wales at Westminster 'by five symbols, to wit by the delivery of a golden rod, by a kiss, by a coronet, by a ring, and by letters of creation'. This is the first time a kiss is mentioned as part of the investiture ceremony.

Harry Monmouth directed the English campaigns against his native rival prince Owain Glyndŵr: a battle between Glyndŵr and the English forces, from a manuscript of about 1485-90 (By permission of the British Library, Cotton Ms. Julius E IV, Art.6, f.1).

Harry Monmouth as prince of Wales (By permission of the British Library, Arundel Ms. 38, f. 37).

Henry IV's reign proved a troubled one, not least because of the national uprising led by Owain Glyndŵr ('Owen Glendower'), a Welsh nobleman of princely ancestry. Beginning in 1400, this revolt continued intermittently for nearly a decade, despite expedition after English expedition sent to crush it. As prince, young Henry was involved in the fighting from the outset. He may have visited Caernarfon Castle with his father in October 1400, and in the following year lost many of his horses and tents when Glyndŵr swooped down from the mountains and ambushed his baggage train. In 1403 he retaliated by burning Owain's home in the Dee valley and (though not yet sixteen) fought his first major battle at Shrewsbury against English rebels under Henry Percy, the famous 'Hotspur'. The prince was there severely wounded in the face by an arrow, but refused to leave the field until victory was won.

The succeeding years saw Glyndŵr and his French allies besieging Caernarfon and controlling much of Wales, of which Owain declared himself independent sovereign prince. Now in personal control of operations, his rival English prince finally began to make headway against him in 1408, when he used heavy siege cannon (for the first time in Wales) to take Aberystwyth Castle. Next year Glyndŵr's last stronghold of Harlech Castle fell to the English prince's forces, and the Welsh prince disappeared into hiding, never to be seen again.

A tall slim young man with a long handsome face and the 'pudding basin' haircut familiar from portraits, Henry loved books, became the first monarch to write letters in English rather than Norman-French, and played the harp for pleasure. Yet Shakespeare's depiction of 'Prince Hal' as a wild youth seems also to have some foundation, as does the tradition that he abruptly reformed his ways when he succeeded as King Henry V in 1413. All the same, 'Harry Monmouth' did not forget his comrades of the 'Glendower War' when he embarked on his career as the most devastatingly successful English warrior king of the Middle Ages. Knights and esquires from Wales and the borders served as his bodyguard at the famous victory of Agincourt (1415), among them Dafydd Gam ('Davy Gam'), knighted as he lay dying on the battlefield.

Having conquered much of France and married the French king's daughter, Henry himself died of raging dysentery in 1422, just before his thirty-fifth birthday. The succession of his baby son, Henry VI, began the train of events which led to the Wars of the Roses, and to a series of tragically short-lived princes of Wales.

Left: *Edward of Lancaster, fifth prince of Wales, was slain at the battle of Tewkesbury in 1471, as depicted here in a French manuscript illustration (By permission of the Library of the University of Ghent, Ms. 236, f.5r).*

Edward of Lancaster

Edward, fifth Prince of Wales 1454-71
Anne Neville, Princess of Wales 1470-71

Edward was born at Westminster in October 1453, the only son of poor King Henry VI and Queen Margaret of Anjou. Sunk deep into madness, the king did not recognize him until he was over a year old, by which time he had already been created nominal prince of Wales. Thenceforward his short life was dominated by his formidable and fiercely protective mother, the real leader of the Lancastrian party in the 'Wars of the Roses'. Long periods in flight or exile — he spent a few hunted weeks in Wales during 1460 — alternated with brief triumphs, making him a bloodthirsty child. At the age of seven he personally ordered the execution of captured Yorkist lords, and a few years later he was said 'to talk of nothing else but cutting off heads and making war'. Edward himself died on the battlefield of Tewkesbury in May 1471, either killed in flight or more probably murdered in cold blood by the Yorkist victors. He was not yet eighteen.

In December 1470 he had married thirteen year old Anne Neville, daughter of the mighty 'Warwick the Kingmaker' — a purely political match which was probably never consummated. Widowed after a uniquely short period of five months as princess of Wales, Anne later married Richard of Gloucester, afterwards King Richard III. Their son became the seventh prince of Wales.

Below: *Edward of York, sixth prince of Wales, from a late fifteenth-century panel in the south choir aisle, St George's Chapel, Windsor Castle (Reproduced by permission of the Dean and Canons of Windsor).*

The Prince in the Tower

Edward, sixth Prince of Wales 1471-83, afterwards King Edward V 1483

Like his predecessor Edward of Lancaster, Edward of York began his life in troubled times, and ended it tragically. The eldest son of the Yorkist King Edward IV and Queen Elizabeth Woodville, he was born in November 1470 in the sanctuary at Westminster Abbey, where the queen had taken refuge from the Lancastrians who drove her husband into exile. But shortly afterwards King Edward returned to defeat his enemies, oversee the murders of Edward of Lancaster and the mad King Henry VI, and create his own seven month old son prince of Wales in June 1471. He clearly intended the boy to exercise real authority in his principality, and,

when only three, Prince Edward was moved to Ludlow Castle, where his advisers could keep watch on the lawless Welsh borders.

In April 1483 the king died, and the twelve year old Prince — a precociously intelligent child — technically succeeded as Edward V. On his way from Ludlow to London, however, he fell into the hands of his uncle Richard of Gloucester, who sent him to 'await his coronation' in the Tower of London. A few weeks later he was joined there by his younger brother the duke of York, whereupon both boys were declared illegitimate on the specious grounds that their parents had not been legally married. On 6 July Gloucester himself was crowned as King Richard III, and soon afterwards the 'Princes in the Tower' disappeared from view. Bones found in the Tower in 1674 (and examined in 1933) may well have been theirs, and there seems little reason to doubt what most people believed at the time, namely that they were murdered on the orders of Richard III.

Edward of Middleham

Edward, seventh Prince of Wales 1483-84

Last and shortest lived of the Plantagenet princes, Edward was the only child of Richard, duke of Gloucester, and Duchess Anne Neville (widow of the fifth prince): he was born at Middleham Castle in Yorkshire, probably in 1476. Soon after his father's usurpation of the throne as Richard III he was created prince of Wales, being invested with a golden coronet and rod during a magnificent ceremony in York Minster on 8 September 1483. Always a sickly child, he survived his investiture by only six months, dying in April 1484: a tomb in Sheriff Hutton church near York may be his. His grief-stricken parents did not long outlive him. Anne died in March 1485 and King Richard in the following August, defeated and slain at Bosworth Field by Henry VII, first of the Tudors.

A Plantagenet family portrait from the Rous Roll. Princess Anne Neville (left), widow of Edward of Lancaster, with her second husband Richard III, and their son Prince Edward of Middleham (right), seventh prince of Wales (By permission of the British Library, Additional Ms. 48976, nos. 62-4).

The Tudor Princes

Arthur, eighth Prince of Wales 1489-1502
Catherine of Aragon, Princess of Wales 1501-02, afterwards Queen of England 1509-36
Henry, ninth Prince of Wales 1504-09, afterwards King Henry VIII 1509-47

Prince Arthur was the embodiment of many hopes and prophecies. From his father, Henry VII, he inherited the Welsh noble blood of the Tudor family, and the English royal blood of the House of Lancaster: while through his mother Queen Elizabeth (Edward IV's daughter) he was also the heir of the royal House of York. His birth on 19 September 1486 therefore sealed the union of the two warring royal families, and brought hope of reconciling the old feud between Welsh and English. The ancient English capital of Winchester was chosen as his birthplace, and the momentousness of the event was further emphasized by naming him after King Arthur, the legendary hero believed once to have ruled all Britain.

Thereafter pageantry and symbolism surrounded every major event of his short, carefully-guarded life. Created prince of Wales at Westminster on 29 November 1489, in 1501 his marriage to the Spanish Princess Catherine of Aragon was accompanied by over a week of shows, tournaments and festivities on a scale never seen before. Arthur himself, however, was too frail to take much part. A slight, blond, bookish boy, his health was always precarious, and many doubted that he was ready to take on the duties either of a husband or a prince of Wales. All the same, after their wedding the teenage couple set up house together at Ludlow Castle on the Welsh border. Five months later, on 2 April 1502, Arthur died there of 'consumption', and was buried in a magnificent tomb-chapel in Worcester Cathedral.

Princess Catherine, left a widow of sixteen, was a grey-eyed, gravely beautiful girl. The daughter of King Ferdinand and Queen Isabella, (the 'Catholic Monarchs' who drove the Moors from Spain and launched Columbus on his voyage of discovery), she represented a marriage alliance which neither England nor Spain could afford to abandon. She was therefore betrothed to Arthur's brother Henry (below) and eventually married him soon after his accession as Henry VIII in 1509. Something of a love-match at first, their marriage turned sour when it failed to produce a male heir, and Henry rejected her for Anne Boleyn. Catherine died in 1536, refusing to accept the legality of the divorce and proclaiming her love for Henry to the last.

Born at Greenwich in 1491, Henry succeeded his brother as prince of Wales in February 1504.

Prince Arthur, eighth prince of Wales, from a portrait by an unknown artist (By gracious permission of Her Majesty the Queen).

Catherine of Aragon, princess of Wales, by Michiel Sittow (By permission of the Kunsthistoriches Museum, Vienna).

A portrait of Henry VIII: the work of an unknown artist about 1520 (By courtesy of the National Portrait Gallery).

A striking contrast both with the delicate Arthur and the tyrannical, overweight monarch he himself later became, Prince Henry dazzled contemporaries with his splendid physique and auburn-haired, fresh-faced good looks: the Venetian ambassador called him 'the handsomest potentate I have ever set eyes on'. He was also a brilliant jouster, something of an intellectual, and a really gifted musician, whose songs are still sung.

During his time as prince some of the anti-Welsh laws passed by earlier English kings were repealed, and towards the end of his reign as

Henry VIII the foundations of modern Wales were laid by the Acts of Union (1536 and 1542/43) with England. But Henry's only son, Edward VI, was never created prince of Wales, and neither Edward nor his royal sisters Mary and Elizabeth had any children. So more than a century would pass before Wales had another Prince.

The Stuart Princes

Henry, tenth Prince of Wales 1610-12
Charles, eleventh Prince of Wales 1616-25, afterwards King Charles I 1625-49
Charles, twelfth Prince of Wales 1638-49, afterwards King Charles II 1649-85
James Edward, nominal Prince of Wales 1688-1701

'The ideal monarch Britain never had', Henry Stuart was born at Stirling Castle in February 1594, the eldest son of King James VI of Scotland and Queen Anne of Denmark. Nine years later his father became James I of England as well, and Henry thus became heir to both kingdoms. He was immediately popular with an English public who had seen no royal children for over half a century, and by the time he was created prince of Wales in June 1610 their admiration bordered on worship. An accomplished sportsman, zealous Protestant, and leading patron of the arts, the personally rather cold and priggish prince soon gathered round him a court which was a model of virtue and order, a glaring contrast with the sordid, drunken, chaotic court of his father King James. Then, quite suddenly, the robust eighteen year old contracted typhoid fever, dying on 6 November 1612 amid universal lamentation. 'Our Rising Sun has set, ere scarcely he had shone', mourned one eulogist, and another called him 'A Jewel whom God only showed the world, we being unworthy to possess him'.

Henry was a hard act to follow, and four years passed before King James consented to create his second son, Charles, prince of Wales. The lacklustre ceremony on 3 November 1616 was to be the last formal investiture until modern times. Born in 1600 in Dunfermline, Charles was a sickly child, with ricketty legs and a nervous stutter he never quite lost. His youth was overshadowed by his dazzling brother, and his early manhood by his father's favourite the duke of Buckingham, who called him 'Baby Charles'. His greatest adventure as prince was travelling disguised to Madrid in 1623 to woo the king of Spain's daughter, a mission which ended in total failure.

Eighteen months later in 1625 he succeeded as King Charles I, a cultivated, withdrawn yet authoritarian monarch, whose tragic conviction that he ruled by Divine Right brought him to the scaffold in 1649, after seven years of Civil Wars against his parliament. During these struggles loyal Welshmen were the backbone of his infantry, and in 1645 he spent several weeks in south and mid-Wales.

Charles I as prince of Wales, about 1617-20, attributed to Abraham van Blyenberch (By courtesy of the National Portrait Gallery).

Henry Frederick Stuart invested as prince of Wales by James I in 1610: a detail from his charter of creation (By permission of the British Library, Additional Ms. 36932).

The ideal prince: a portrait of Henry Frederick by Robert Peake, about 1611 (The Collection at Parham Park, Sussex).

The king's eldest son Charles, born in London in May 1630, was known as prince of Wales from the spring of 1638. A brave, early-maturing boy, during the first Civil War (1642-46) he nominally commanded a troop of cavalry decked with his ostrich-plume badge, and after his father's execution invaded England to claim the throne as Charles II. Defeated by Cromwell at Worcester in 1651, the unusually tall and swarthy Charles ('a tall black man over two yards high') was forced to hide from his enemies in an oak tree, before fleeing into penniless exile until his triumphant Restoration in 1660.

Charles, twelfth prince of Wales at the age of twelve, afterwards King Charles II: a portrait by William Dobson (By permission of the Scottish National Portrait Gallery).

Though this attractive and intelligent monarch fathered at least twelve children by seven mistresses (including the Welsh Lucy Walter), he had no legitimate offspring. It was therefore left to his unpopular Roman Catholic brother King James II (1685- 88) to produce the next potential prince of Wales. Born on 10 June 1688, his only son James Edward was proclaimed prince soon after birth, but those who feared a Catholic succession spread the rumour that the baby was really the child of unknown parents, smuggled into the queen's bed in a warming pan. Six months later, the baby prince and his deposed father took refuge in France, where James Edward was proclaimed 'King James III' on his father's death in 1701. More commonly known as 'The Old Pretender', he died in 1766, by which time four successive Hanoverian princes of Wales (descendants of James I's daughter) had been created in Britain.

'The Warming Pan Prince'. James Edward Stuart, nominal prince of Wales, by François de Troy (By permission of the Scottish National Portrait Gallery).

The Hanoverian Princes

George Augustus, thirteenth Prince of Wales 1714-27, afterwards King George II 1727-60
Caroline of Anspach, Princess of Wales 1714-27, afterwards Queen 1727-34
Frederick, fourteenth Prince of Wales 1729-51
Augusta of Saxe-Gotha, Princess of Wales 1736-72
George William, fifteenth Prince of Wales 1751-60, afterwards King George III 1760-1820

George I, great-grandson of James I and the first of the Hanoverian kings, arrived in London from his native Germany on 21 September 1714, and on the very next day created his son George Augustus prince of Wales. Born at Herrenhausen in Hanover in November 1683, the new prince was already nearly thirty-one, and already married to Caroline of Anspach, a big blonde German beauty who thus became the first princess of Wales for more than two centuries. She was far cleverer than her loving, unimaginative, unintellectual husband — who once declared, in his execrable German accent, 'I hate all boets and bainters'. Yet the dapper,

George Augustus, thirteenth prince of Wales, afterwards King George II. Portrait by Sir Godfrey Kneller (By gracious permission of Her Majesty the Queen).

pop-eyed, red-faced prince had many good qualities, not least the bravery he displayed in Marlborough's wars: he liked the English and they liked him, while the London Welsh made him president of their 'Society of Ancient Britons'. Indeed, his new subjects much preferred him to his ungracious father, with whom (like all Hanoverian princes) he was on chronically bad terms, and who once planned to have him kidnapped and deported to America.

The prince succeeded as George II in 1727, and became the last British monarch personally to lead his troops into battle, at Dettingen in 1743. On 9 June 1729 he created his own eldest son Frederick prince of Wales, albeit with a very bad grace, for both king and queen loathed and detested 'Poor Fred', as he was generally known. Born in Hanover in 1707, the sallow, undersized prince could be generous and charming, and had cultivated tastes in art and music. His mother, however, publicly called him 'the greatest ass and the greatest liar and the greatest beast in the whole world', and wished the earth would swallow him. 'Frederick's popularity', she declared, 'makes me vomit'. Poor Fred retaliated by heading the political opposition to his parents, who viewed his death in March 1751 (of an abscess caused by a blow from a tennis ball) with considerable relief, while an anonymous wit wrote:

'Here lies Poor Fred
Who was alive and is dead
There's no more to be said'.

The next prince of Wales, created with unseemly haste less than a month after his father's death, was George William, 'Poor Fred's' eldest son by his gawky, formidable wife Augusta of Saxe-Gotha. Born in London in 1738, George was a shy, serious boy, completely dominated by his mother 'The Princess Dowager' and her odious adviser the earl of Bute, an influence which persisted after the death of his royal grandfather and his accession as George III in 1760. Much more English than his predecessors, 'Farmer George' made a good if somewhat narrow- minded monarch for his troubled times, though from 1788 he suffered intermittently from porphyria, the 'royal malady' inherited from the Stuarts which plunged him irretrievably into madness in 1810. Thereafter, royal power was exercised by one of the most famous princes of Wales, his son George 'the Prince Regent'.

'A shy, serious boy'. George, fifteenth prince of Wales, and later King George III, by Jean-Etienne Liotard (By gracious permission of Her Majesty the Queen).

Below: *'A big, blonde German beauty'. Princess Caroline of Anspach, by Sir Godfrey Kneller (By gracious permission of Her Majesty the Queen).*

Bottom: *Princess Augusta of Saxe-Gotha, wife of 'Poor Fred', from a portrait by William Hogarth (By gracious permission of Her Majesty the Queen).*

Prince Frederick Louis, fourteenth prince of Wales, alias 'Poor Fred', with his sisters. A group portrait by Philippe Mercier, 1733 (By courtesy of the National Portrait Gallery).

The Prince Regent

George Augustus Frederick, sixteenth Prince of Wales 1762-1820, afterwards King George IV 1820-30
Caroline of Brunswick, Princes of Wales 1795-1820

Prince of Wales for fifty-eight years, during the last nine of which he was effectively ruler of Britain, George was born at St James's Palace on 12 August 1762 and created prince a week later. He was the first of George III's fifteen children by the plain but amiable Queen Charlotte, and was strictly brought up in the crowded royal nursery at Kew. Though a clever and likeable boy, by his late teens he was already following the Hanoverian tradition of quarrelling with his father, who disapproved strongly of George's drinking, gambling and multifarious love affairs.

These temporarily ceased in 1784, when he fell in love with Mrs Maria Fitzherbert, a virtuous Roman Catholic widow six years his senior: since she refused to become his mistress, he secretly but quite legally married her in 1785, despite the fact that the Royal Marriages Act forbade such unions with Roman Catholics. Ten years later, however, he himself decided the marriage was invalid, and in the hope of paying his enormous debts married his flighty cousin Princess Caroline of Brunswick.

Their union was disastrous from the outset. Greeted on landing by the prince's current mistress, his new bride thought George 'Very fat, and nothing like his portrait'. He, in turn, appeared at the wedding 'like a condemned man' and extremely drunk, whereafter they lived together for less than a month before separating. During the next twenty-five years he tried unavailingly to divorce 'this so-called Princess of Wales', whose own behaviour grew increasingly more scandalous and eccentric.

Meanwhile, the witty and extravagant prince established a reputation as 'the First Gentleman of Europe'. His racing stables alone cost more than half his official annual income, and the perfection of his fashionable wardrobe was breathtaking. He thought nothing of ordering thirty waistcoats a month, even his bathing suits were lined in silk or 'finest Welsh flannel', and he spent fortunes on perfumed wig powder, sent thirty-six pounds at a time. The corpulence which nicknamed him 'the Prince of Whales', however, was partially the result of enforced inactivity. For despite his father's intermittent bouts of mental illness, George was allowed no real power or responsibility until the old king's final breakdown in 1810, when he was appointed Prince Regent.

George's own genuine good taste left its mark on the 'Regency' era that followed: apart from

'The Prince of Whales'. Caricature of the Prince Regent by James Gillray (By courtesy of the National Portrait Gallery).

'The First Gentleman of Europe'. The young and slender Prince George, sixteenth prince of Wales, by George Stubbs. The prince's racing stables alone cost more than half his official annual income (By gracious permission of Her Majesty the Queen).

his beloved Brighton Pavilion, he also commissioned Buckingham Palace and extensive alterations to Windsor Castle. In January 1820 he at last succeeded as King George IV, whereafter a final attempt to divorce the temporarily popular 'Queen' Caroline prompted a near-revolution in London. Her spirit broken by forcible exclusion from his Coronation in 1821, she died three weeks later. The king heard the news during his only visit to Wales, a fleeting call on the marquess of Anglesey (then constable of Caernarfon Castle) at Plas Newydd in Anglesey, while sailing to Ireland. He himself died of dropsy on 26 June 1830: at his own request, he was buried with a miniature of Mrs Fitzherbert, 'the real princess of Wales'.

The wedding of Prince George and Caroline of Brunswick by Henry Singleton. Neither partner looks enthusiastic, and the marriage proved disastrous (By gracious permission of Her Majesty the Queen).

Edward and Alexandra

Albert Edward, seventeenth Prince of Wales 1841-1901, afterwards Kind Edward VII 1901-10
Alexandra of Denmark, Princess of Wales 1863-1901, afterwards Queen Alexandra 1901-10

Albert Edward, eldest son of Queen Victoria and her idolized husband Prince Albert, was born at Buckingham Palace on 8 November 1841, and created prince some three weeks later: he was destined to become the longest-serving of all princes of Wales, holding the title for nearly sixty years. Anxious to check any tendency to imitate the Prince Regent or the queen's other Hanoverian 'wicked uncles', his parents had him brought up very strictly. But their programme of unrelenting academic work, rigid supervision and stern seclusion proved totally counter-productive. For instead of following the example of the serious, moral Albert ('that perfection of human beings'), 'Prince Bertie' developed into a pleasure-loving socialite, whose escapades consistently failed to amuse his formidable mother.

Prince Albert Edward and Princess Alexandra, with their son Albert Victor (Copyright: The Hulton-Deutsch Collection).

After the prince's youthful adventure with an actress — which the queen believed to have hastened his father's premature death in 1861 — it was decided that he must marry. The bride selected was the 'outrageously pretty' Princess Alexandra of Denmark (1844-1925), whom he wedded in 1863, at a magnificent ceremony scarcely dampened by the queen's insistence on wearing black, or the tantrums of his four year old nephew, the future German Kaiser Wilhelm II. Wildly popular from the first, 'Princess Alix' retained her beauty, gaiety and sense of humour throughout her life: her faultless dress-sense made her a leader of fashion, and even her 'Alexandra limp' (contracted during an illness in 1867) was widely imitated. An animal-lover who once adopted an Egyptian sheep intended for her dinner, she was hopelessly unpunctual, being very nearly late for her own coronation in 1902. Nor did she allow the prince's 'other ladies' — including the actresses Lily Langtry and Sarah Bernhardt and the socialites Lady Brooke and Mrs Keppel — to affect the happiness of their marriage.

The Victorian public were less tolerant. An outcry against the prince's involvement in a divorce case was defused by his serious illness in 1872, but the 'Baccarat Scandal' of 1891 damaged his reputation, as did his liking for raffish company and his hectic social life. This centred on the estate he purchased at Sandringham in Norfolk (where he indulged his passion for shooting) and frequent trips to European resorts like Paris, Biarritz and Marienbad. He was also famous for his gargantuan appetite (provoking the highly unofficial nickname 'Tum-Tum'), his huge cigars, and his promotion of new fashions like the dinner-jacket, the Homburg hat, the Norfolk jacket, and the habit (necessary in his case) of leaving the lowest waistcoat button undone.

'The presentation of an address from the north Wales people to the prince and princess of Wales in the upper castle-yard, Carnarvon Castle', on the occasion of their visit in 1868 (Copyright: The Illustrated London News Picture Library).

Below: *The arms of Prince Albert Edward, inserted into a window opening in the Eagle Tower at Caernarfon during restoration of the castle under the direction of Sir Llewelyn Turner* *(see p. 37).*

Though Queen Victoria steadfastly refused to allow him any public responsibility, she could not check his love of travel. The first member of the British royal family to visit the United States of America, in 1868 he became the first prince of Wales to visit Caernarfon Castle for nearly five centuries. He and Princess Alexandra came again in 1894, for the National Eisteddfod, and he visited once more in 1907.

By that time he had at last succeeded as King Edward VII (on 22 January 1901). By then, too, public opinion had grown less censorious, and he made a good and popular monarch at home, while his influence abroad did much to maintain the fragile stability of Europe. 'Edward the Peacemaker' died sincerely mourned in 1910, and for many his 'Edwardian Age' would seem a golden Indian Summer before the horrors of the First World War.

The Sailor Prince

George, eighteenth Prince of Wales 1901-10, afterwards King George V 1910-36
Mary of Teck, Princess of Wales 1901-10, afterwards Queen Mary 1910-36

On 3 June 1865, a second son was born to Prince Edward and Princess Alexandra at Marlborough House, London. Although Queen Victoria inevitably insisted that 'Albert' be included among his names, the boy was always known as 'George'. His happy, boisterous upbringing was very different from that of his father, who had no wish either to inflict the strict regime of his own youth on his children, or to perpetuate the sad tradition that royal heirs must always quarrel with their parents. Nor did Prince George seem likely to inherit the responsibilities of rule, which would fall to his elder brother, the amiable but (as it increasingly appeared) incurably listless Prince Albert Victor, known as 'Prince Eddie'.

Instead, George embarked at the age of twelve on the life of a dedicated career naval officer, gaining his first independent command (a fast torpedo-boat) in 1889. Just over two years later, however, Prince Eddie died suddenly of pneumonia, leaving his brother his place in the succession. Now created duke of York, it also seemed entirely appropriate that George should marry the bride Queen Victoria had chosen for Prince Eddie, the serious and capable English-educated Princess Mary ('May') of Teck (1867-1953). After a somewhat hesitant courtship the pair were married in 1893: their union was to prove supremely happy.

The great matriarch Victoria died in January 1901, when George became heir to his father Edward VII's throne. Nearly a year passed, however, before he was created prince of Wales on his father's sixtieth birthday (9 November 1901), as a reward for his arduous 45,000 mile (72,400km) tour of the Commonwealth. Thereafter, breaking the long-established mould of hostility between monarchs and princes, father and son worked closely together, and Prince George was entrusted with many responsibilities and delicate missions. He succeeded as King George V in 1910, always remaining at heart a straightforward, honourable and uncomplicated naval officer. Having led his nation through a horrific World War, he made the first Royal Christmas broadcast in 1932, and laid the foundations of the present affectionate relations between monarchy and people.

His reign also saw a momentous development in the story of Caernarfon Castle. In 1875 George had visited the castle as a child: he returned as duke of York in 1899, and again as prince in 1902, when he became chancellor of the University of Wales. His post-Coronation visit in July 1911, however, was marked by a ceremony which had lapsed since early Stuart times — the formal investiture of his eldest son as prince of Wales, now performed for the first time in the castle where the original English title-holder had been born more than six centuries before.

In 1902 Prince George, eighteenth prince of Wales, was installed as chancellor of the University of Wales at Caernarfon Castle. Here he is seen at the same ceremony, conferring the degree of Doctor of Music upon Princess Alexandra, the princess of Wales (Copyright: The Illustrated London News Picture Library).

Sir John de Havering (Constable 1284-c.1300)

Sir Otto de Grandison (Constable c.1286-92)

Roger Mortimer of Chirk (Constable 1316-22)

Edmund, earl of Arundel (Constable 1322-26)

Sir William Bagot (Constable c.1390-97)

The Constables of Caernarfon

The ceremonial key and great padlock to Caernarfon Castle. The key itself was offered to Queen Elizabeth II by the earl of Snowdon, in his role as constable, at the Investiture of His Royal Highness Prince Charles in 1969.

However strongly-built, beautiful or symbolic a castle may be — and Caernarfon is certainly all of these — it is quite useless without soldiers to defend it. Almost as soon as Caernarfon's foundations were laid, therefore, a royal official was appointed to take charge of its defence: his name was Thomas de Maydenhacche, and his title — one borne in an unbroken line up to the present day — was constable of Caernarfon. Probably the first effective constable, however, was the tough Essex knight Sir John de Havering, who in October 1284 was ordered to recruit the castle's first garrison of forty men. At least fifteen of these were to be armed with deadly crossbows (then the most effective weapon of defence), and the force was also to include night watchmen and gatekeepers, as well as a chaplain, a carpenter, and an armourer to maintain its weapons.

Another important early constable was Sir Otto de Grandison, a 'Savoyard' knight (from what is now Switzerland) who was King Edward I's lifelong friend and confidant. Indeed, the king once declared that 'there was no-one about him who could do his will better: nay, it could not be better done if he were to attend to it himself in person'. Hence Edward made Grandison his 'justiciar' or personal viceroy in conquered north Wales, with a headquarters at Caernarfon Castle and special charge over the building and defence of all the new royal fortresses in Wales. But crusading and diplomacy often took Sir Otto abroad, and it was left to Sir John de Havering to pick up the pieces after the disastrous Welsh attack of 1294 (see p. 45). A year later he was standing guard over the rebuilding work with a much increased garrison of twenty fully-equipped men-at-arms, forty crossbowmen, and a hundred foot soldiers.

Though there would be no more Welsh assaults on Caernarfon for over a century, it remained vitally important to the rulers of England that their great royal palace, fortress and administrative centre should remain securely in the hands of men they could trust. The list of constables of Caernarfon during the fourteenth and fifteenth centuries is therefore a barometer of the political disputes and civil wars of those unsettled times. In 1322, for example, Edward II removed his opponent Roger Mortimer of Chirk from the office, substituting his ally the earl of Arundel: but four years later the victorious Mortimers cut off Arundel's head, making their agent William Shalford constable in his stead. Then, in the last years of the fourteenth century, Richard II appointed his favourites Sir William Bagot (of Shakespeare's 'Bushy, Bagot and Green') and William le Scrope, earl of Wiltshire, as successive constables: but Richard's deposer Henry IV executed Scrope, substituting the appropriately-named John Bolde, who afterwards defended Caernarfon against Owain Glyndŵr (see p. 46).

Sir William le Scrope (Constable 1397-99)

Sir Thomas Montgomery (Constable 1461-83)

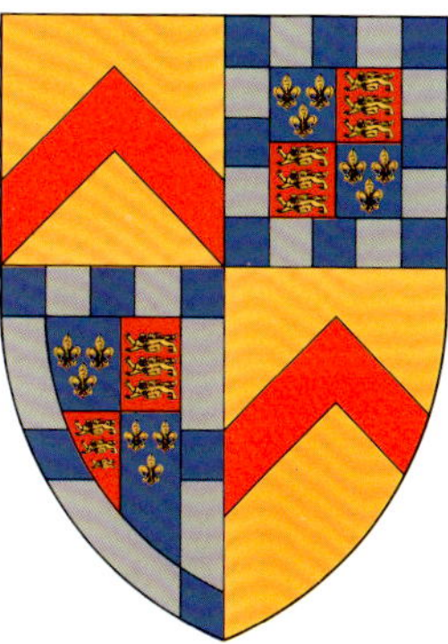

Henry Stafford, duke of Buckingham (Constable 1483-84)

Sir William Stanley (Constable 1481-95)

Charles Brandon, duke of Suffolk (Constable 1509-c.1516)

The vast upper ward of the castle. The Welsh slate dais formed the centre of a huge 'theatrical set' designed under the direction of the earl of Snowdon for the Investiture of Prince Charles in 1969 (see p. 40). In fact, the dais stands near the centre of the earliest Norman castle at Caernarfon — a massive earthwork which dictated the shape of King Edward I's stronghold at this point.

Above: *'A dashing horse soldier': the heroic Lord Uxbridge, first marquess of Anglesey, longest-serving of Caernarfon's constables (1812-54). A portrait by R. T. Bott, 1839 (By permission of The National Trust).*

Above Left: *'Bloody Boasting Byron': John, Lord Byron, the last fighting constable of Caernarfon. The wound on his cheek was received in a skirmish in January 1643. A portrait by William Dobson (By courtesy of the University of Manchester, Tabley House Collection — photograph by the Courtauld Institute of Art).*

Later, at the height of the Wars of the Roses, the Yorkist King Edward IV removed the long-serving Lancastrian Constable Jenkyn Stanley (1427-60), putting in his own reliable supporter Sir Thomas Montgomery (1461-83). Almost as soon as Edward was dead, however, Richard III secured Caernarfon by entrusting it to his henchman Henry duke of Buckingham and, after Buckingham turned against him, transferring it to the supposedly more reliable Sir William Stanley. His judgement proved wrong again, for scarcely a year later Stanley led the charge that slew Richard at Bosworth, and settled down to hold the castle for the new King Henry VII.

With the more peaceful rule of the Tudors, and the progressive dilapidation of the castle, the post of constable became increasingly an honorary one, held among many others by Henry VIII's friend and brother-in-law Charles Brandon, duke of Suffolk (constable 1509-*c*.1516). But the Civil Wars between Charles I and parliament again brought the castle's defensive role into play, and its last fighting constable was the cavalier John Lord Byron (nicknamed 'Bloody Boasting Byron'), who finally surrendered Caernarfon to the parliamentarian General Mytton in 1646.

Thereafter the castle became a picturesque ruin, and the duties of its constable more or less nominal — though the office was still much sought after. During the later seventeenth and early eighteenth centuries it was held by the family of the earls of Radnor, of Cornish origin despite their Welsh title. In 1724, however, George prince of Wales granted the constableship to a local man, Thomas Wynn of Glynnllivon Castle, five miles (8km) south of Caernarfon town. His descendants held it for three generations, being superseded by the Paget earls of Uxbridge, of Plas Newydd across the Menai Strait in Anglesey.

The fourth earl of Uxbridge, granted the office in 1812, was much the most flamboyant of the later constables. A dashing horse soldier, he commanded Wellington's cavalry at the battle of Waterloo in 1815, where one of the last shots fired shattered his knee. 'By God, Sir, I've lost my leg', he is said to have cried, to which the laconic Wellington replied, 'By God, Sir, so you have'. Later in the day the leg was amputated, and though no anaesthetic was used Uxbridge merely remarked that he thought the saw rather blunt. Eye witnesses confirmed that his pulse never quickened throughout. Some years afterwards, created marquess of Anglesey for his services, he returned to the scene of the operation, and insisted on dining from the table on which it had occurred: he died in 1854 aged 86, the longest-serving of all Caernarfon's constables.

His successors included the ninth earl of Caernarvon (constable 1854-90), whose deputy constable Sir Llewelyn Turner carried out extensive repairs to the castle; the great Welsh politician David Lloyd George, who master-minded the Investiture of Prince Edward in 1911; and the fourth earl of Harlech (constable 1945-63), who carried the standard of Wales at Queen Elizabeth II's coronation. The present constable, the successor of more than fifty who have held office in unbroken succession from Thomas de Maydenhacche, is Antony Armstrong-Jones, earl of Snowdon.

Deputy-Constable Sir Llewelyn Turner (1823-1903), who directed the work of restoration at the castle in late Victorian times.

The present constable, the earl of Snowdon, receives the Queen for the Investiture of Prince Charles, 1969 (Copyright: The Hulton-Deutsch Collection).

The Earldom of Chester

Every English prince of Wales from Edward of Caernarfon to Charles has also been earl of Chester, a title generally but not always granted at the same time as the principality. The earldom is a very ancient one. It originated soon after the Norman Conquest, when William the Conqueror made Chester a 'county palatine' whose earls had virtually the same powers as a king within the area they governed. The purpose of creating this 'kingdom within a kingdom' was to establish the border county of Cheshire as a strong buffer-state between England and the yet unconquered Welsh, as well as a secure base for extending the rule of the English monarchs into Wales itself. It was the first Norman earl of Chester, indeed, who raised the earliest medieval castle at Caernarfon, on the site of King Edward I's present great fortress-palace.

The last semi-independent Norman earl of Chester died in 1237, whereafter the county was acquired by King Henry III. Since then the earldom has remained an exclusively royal title, first granted by King Henry to his son Prince Edward (later Edward I) in 1254, then by Edward I to Edward of Caernarfon in 1301, and thenceforward to the eldest son of nearly every English monarch. Yet the 'county palatine' of Chester long retained its separate character, and was not even represented in English parliaments until 1541. It remains proud of its special relationship with the princes of Wales, in token of which the mayor of Chester led the procession of civic dignitaries during Prince Charles's Investiture at Caernarfon in 1969.

The seal of Ranulf de Glanville, earl of Chester (above), *with the corn-sheaves emblem of the earldom* (top).

Royal Investitures

The Investiture of Prince Edward, July 1911

Constable Lloyd George awaits the arrival of King George V outside the Eagle Tower for the 1911 Investiture of Prince Edward. As MP for Caernarfon, Lloyd George was the principal promoter of the ceremony.

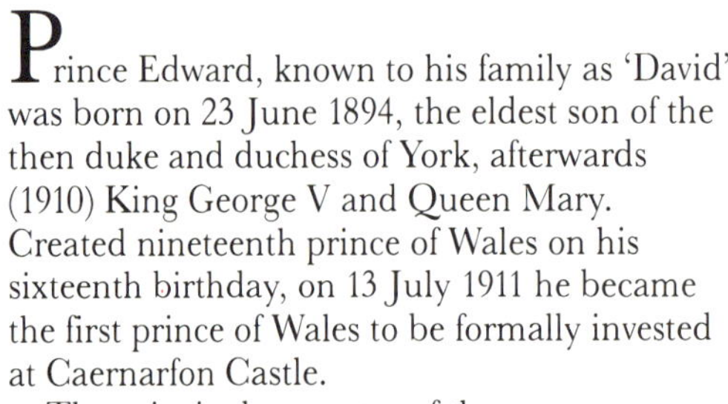

Prince Edward, known to his family as 'David' was born on 23 June 1894, the eldest son of the then duke and duchess of York, afterwards (1910) King George V and Queen Mary. Created nineteenth prince of Wales on his sixteenth birthday, on 13 July 1911 he became the first prince of Wales to be formally invested at Caernarfon Castle.

The principal promoter of the ceremony was David Lloyd George, MP for Caernarfon, constable of Caernarfon castle and — most important — currently chancellor of the exchequer. 'With an eye to what would please his constituents', wrote Prince Edward, Lloyd George also proposed that he should learn some Welsh. 'Mr Lloyd George became my coach in the Welsh language, and I still have, written in his own hand, some of the Welsh sentences he taught me to speak at the investiture. One was 'Môr o gân yw Cymru i gyd', meaning 'All Wales is a sea of song'. Mr Lloyd George made me repeat it over and over again, saying with a twinkle, 'All Welshmen will love you for that'.

Though the prince's Welsh amounted only to three and half sentences, *The Times* at least was impressed by the Welshness of the magnificent occasion. 'For the first time all those in attendance on the prince, and by far the greater proportion of the 10,000 spectators were Welsh.

Part of the 'sea of song' was provided by this 430-strong Caernarvonshire choir. 'The march to the castle of the Welsh choir, the women most picturesque in their red cloaks and steeple-crowned hats' (The Times).

'What would my naval friends say if they saw me in this preposterous rig?': Prince Edward in his regalia as prince of Wales.

For the first time an English prince of Wales addressed his people in their native tongue, the living speech of the populace. And probably for the first time the ceremony of presentation has been performed for the benefit of the people'.

For the prince himself, the experience was a traumatic one, and worst of all were the clothes he had to wear. 'The ceremony I had to go through with, the speech I had to make, and the Welsh I had to speak were, I thought, a sufficient ordeal for anyone. But when a tailor appeared to measure me for a fantastic costume designed for the occasion . . . I decided things had gone too far. What would my naval friends say if they saw me in this preposterous rig? There was a family blow-up that night; but in the end my mother, as always, smoothed things over . . . I also got the impression that if I did what was asked of me, it would help Papa in his dealings with the difficult Mr Lloyd George'. *('A King's Story: Memoirs of the Duke of Windsor')*

In later years Edward became a popular if sometimes controversial 'Prince Charming', and a frequent visitor to Wales. He succeeded as King Edward VIII in January 1936, but was never crowned. His determination to marry the twice-divorced Mrs Simpson led him to abdicate in favour of his brother George VI on 10 December 1936, whereafter he lived abroad as 'Duke of Windsor' until his death in 1972.

Far Right: *The presentation of the prince at the Queen's Gate, greeted by 'a thrilling outburst of acclamations'.*

Right: *The special Investiture issue of the magazine* Wales, *July 1911.*

Below: *The prince of Wales after the Investiture, thanked by King George V and Queen Mary. The queen thought 'David looked charming in his purple and minever cloak and gold circlet, and did his part very well. The heat was awful'.*

The Investiture of Prince Charles

Charles Philip Arthur George, the present prince of Wales, was born at Buckingham Palace on 14 November 1948, the eldest son of Princess Elizabeth (now Queen Elizabeth II) and Prince Philip, duke of Edinburgh. On the death of his grandfather George VI in 1952 he became heir to the throne, and on 26 July 1958 he was created prince of Wales in an entirely novel manner. On that day tens of thousands of people had packed Cardiff Arms Park for the closing ceremony of the British Empire and Commonwealth Games. To them, and 'to all Welsh people wherever they may be', the tape-recorded and broadcast voice of the queen — unavoidably absent due to a minor operation — quite unexpectedly announced that 'I intend to create my son Charles prince of Wales today. When he is grown up, I will present him to you at Caernarfon'.

4-PAGE EXTRA
Your usual WESTERN MAIL is inside

WESTERN MAIL

GAMES SPECIAL

Commonwealth shares a day of history ★ The Queen gives news all Wales had awaited

THE CROWNING MOMENT

43,000 crowd cheer Games climax

By Ena Kendall

PRINCE CHARLES IS TO BE CREATED PRINCE OF WALES. THESE WERE THE WORDS, RECORDED BY THE QUEEN, WHICH RAISED EXCITEMENT TO FEVER PITCH AT THE TRIUMPHANT CLOSING CEREMONY OF THE SIXTH BRITISH EMPIRE AND COMMONWEALTH GAMES AT CARDIFF ARMS PARK ON SATURDAY.

The Western Mail *breaks the news of Prince Charles's creation as prince of Wales, two days after the official announcement, 28 July 1958.*

The Investiture of Prince Charles in the upper ward of the castle, 1969.

The prince kneels at the moment of Investiture.

The promised Investiture and presentation took place on 1 July 1969, and in many ways followed the precedents set at Prince Edward's Investiture forty-eight years before. The staff, ring and sword of office, wrought in Caernarvonshire gold, were those used in 1911: though a new and more elaborate coronet was designed, and poor Prince Edward's 'preposterous rig' was replaced by Prince Charles's far more dignified uniform of the Royal Regiment of Wales. The processions of peers and MPs, mayors and high sheriffs, bards and druids were seen again, along with the indispensable Welsh choir and military bands: though this time there was also a fly-past of RAF jets.

Yet the differences between the two ceremonies were also marked, and perhaps more significant. The staging of the 1969 Investiture, devised by the constable, Lord Snowdon, was far more spectacular, ambitious — and modern, down to the expanded polystyrene red dragons on the ceremonial banners. It transformed the castle courtyard into an immense 'theatre in the round', ringed with flame-red seating and centred upon three thrones of riven Welsh slate on a circular slate dais, beneath a soaring transparent canopy decked with the prince of Wales's feathers. Not to be left out, Caernarfon town also underwent a rejuvenating facelift. A local firm had offered free paint to any householder who would abide by the overall supervision of a professor from the Welsh School of Architecture, and now the town blossomed out in the reds, blues and yellows of royal heraldry.

The royal procession enters the castle from the Eagle Tower, with Queen Elizabeth II and Prince Philip, duke of Edinburgh, in the foreground.

The regalia worn by Prince Charles. The coronet was designed by architect and artist Louis Osman.

Nor was all this colour and spectacle enjoyed only by those present at Caernarfon on the day of the Investiture. A mere 10,000 spectators had witnessed the 1911 ceremony, but the international audience of the 1969 event — the world's first major colour television outside broadcast — is said to have numbered some 200 million. It included the seventy-five year old Edward, duke of Windsor — the focus of the 1911 Investiture — who watched the installation of his successor on television in his Paris home.

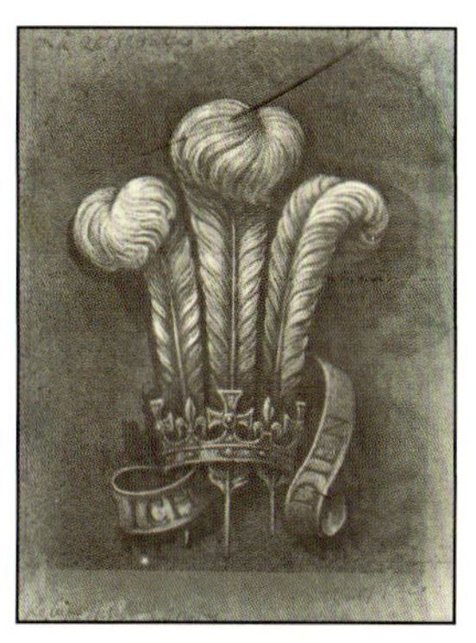

Carl Toms's design for the prince of Wales's feathers which graced the canopy and King's Gate at the Investiture was a less formal, more 'romantic' depiction than that traditionally associated with the princes of Wales.

Top: *Carl Toms's initial design for the prince of Wales's three-feathered insignia.*
Middle: *The design is translated into gilded expanded polystyrene feathers which adorn the King's Gate at the castle.*
Bottom: *A graphic representation of the design.*

Probably the most important difference between the two ceremonies, however, was the way in which the princely candidates were prepared. In 1911 Prince Edward's few cosmetic Welsh phrases were thought more than sufficient to content nascent Welsh nationalist sentiments, but by 1969 the situation had altered radically. The announcement of Prince Charles's Investiture had provoked considerable criticism in Wales, and though only a tiny handful of fanatics were prepared to translate their disapproval into a (eventually fatal) bombing campaign, it was at one time feared that the prince's life might really be in danger: by the day of the ceremony, indeed, obituaries and 'personal tributes' had secretly been prepared. The news that the prince was to spend a term studying Welsh at Aberystwyth University was also at first dismissed in some quarters as 'a political stunt'. But three weeks before the Investiture he made a speech in fluent and faultless Welsh, to the highly critical audience at a Welsh Youth Eisteddfod, and all but the most inveterate of his detractors were silenced, or even won over to enthusiasm.

The prince with 'coronet on the head, a ring on the finger, and a rod in hand' begins to leave the castle after the Investiture.

Prince Charles is presented to the people of Wales.

Above: *'Princely souvenirs': the Investiture was cause for great celebration throughout Wales.*

Left: *The royal party leave the castle waving from a landau.*

Below: *Prince Charles and Princess Diana, escorted by the present constable, the earl of Snowdon, on a visit to Caernarfon in 1981.*

'When he stood up at the Eisteddfod and started to speak in Welsh', declared the initially reluctant mayor of Caernarfon, 'he wasn't just a boy. He was a prince. You could have put a suit of armour on that lad, and sent him off to Agincourt'. Gwynfor Evans MP, president of Plaid Cymru (the Welsh Nationalist party) wrote more soberly: 'Prince Charles has won the admiration of most Welsh people by applying himself so successfully to his Welsh studies, and I believe that he now has a genuine interest in Wales'. At the Investiture itself, moreover, Prince Charles replied to the Loyal Address with another speech in Welsh, confirming that he had become the first English prince of Wales ever to speak and understand the native language of his principality.

Twelve years later Prince Charles was back in Caernarfon, this time bringing with him the first princess of Wales for more than seven decades — Princess Diana, whom he married at St Paul's Cathedral on 29 July 1981. It was entirely appropriate that one of the couple's first visits should have been to the great royal palace in Wales, where their son Prince William (born 21 June 1982) may one day be invested as prince of Wales in his turn.

Another Point of View: Caernarfon and the Welsh

An early fourteenth-century seal [cast] of the borough of Caernarfon. The new town was established by King Edward I to service the fortress-palace (By courtesy of the Society of Antiquaries).

The castle and fortified town of Caernarfon were a bitter affront to the Welsh people in whose land they stood. Their intrusion on a site hallowed by ancient Welsh legend was an insult, to which injury was added by the unceremonious demolition of the pre-existing Welsh town of 'Kaerinarvon', swept away to make room for the new defences. As these new defences began to take shape, moreover, it became all too clear that the initial affront could not be ignored: the towering symbols of defeat would remain centres of continuing oppression, which would blight the everyday lives of Welsh men and women for many miles around.

In this respect the new town was perhaps worse than the new castle. Established to service the royal fortress-palace, it was also intended to help 'pacify' and 'civilize' the native Welsh population, or in other words to enforce upon them an alien culture. Its earliest inhabitants — masons, administrators and soldiers, as well as merchants, entrepreneurs and doubtless less respectable hangers-on — were without exception foreigners, Englishmen with a sprinkling of French and Irish, attracted to the

Inset Below Left: *To native Welshmen, Edward I's planted towns were cuckoos in the nest. They were consistent targets for Welsh resentment throughout the fourteenth century. Caernarfon was first seized in open revolt in 1294, and was besieged in the Glyndŵr rebellion in the early 1400s. This fourteenth-century French manuscript illustration shows besiegers surrounding a walled town (By permission of the British Library, Royal Ms. 1 E IX, f.222).*

Main Picture: *The castle and town walls on the edge of the Menai Strait.*

Inset Below Right: *In the Welsh revolt of 1294, anything in the castle or town that would burn was set on fire: an early fourteenth-century manuscript illustration (By permission of the British Library, Royal Ms. 20 A II, f.3).*

new 'frontier-town' by generous privileges as well as the hope of profit. Part of that profit, furthermore, would be made at the expense of the Welsh: for though native Welshmen were forbidden to live in the town, they were strictly prohibited from doing business outside it. If a Welsh trader wanted to sell butter, eggs, or beer, he must do so in Caernarfon market, paying a toll to its alien townsmen for the privilege.

It is scarcely surprising, therefore, that Welshmen resented this fortified cuckoo in their nest; more so that their resentment took ten years to bubble over into revolt. Their attack erupted suddenly and with devastating force, quite unexpected by the 'frontiersmen', though clearly carefully planned by the Welsh. Led by a nobleman called Madog ap Llywelyn, the rebels burst into the town on Michaelmas Day (29 September) 1294, perhaps breaching its western walls near their junction with the castle. 'Suspecting nothing of the kind', many of the inhabitants were enjoying themselves at the Michaelmas Fair: those who could not flee in time were put to the sword, and Roger Puleston, the king's sheriff of Anglesey, was caught and lynched. Next came the turn of the castle, as yet protected on its townward side by little more than a ditch and wooden stockade. This, too, was soon breached and fired, along with the town quay and anything else in town or castle that would burn, and during the next six months the occupying Welsh began systematically demolishing the stone town walls, also doing considerable damage to the castle.

Following the revolt of 1294-95 large sums were spent in repairing and strengthening the castle and town defences. The elaborate defences of the King's Gate reflect the insecurity left by the recent disaster.

When King Edward eventually put down the rebellion — though not before he had himself been virtually besieged in Conwy Castle — Caernarfon town therefore had to be effectively rebuilt, while even stronger defences than originally envisaged were planned for its castle. New English settlers were helped to forget the massacre of their predecessors by the grant of even greater concessions, and reassured by still more draconian anti-Welsh laws. Henceforward, for example, no Welshman might carry arms within the town: for as James of St George, architect of the castle, once remarked, 'the Welsh are the Welsh, and you have to know them well and watch out for them'.

Such racial laws, of course, also served to bank up the fires of native resentment, though more than a century passed before these again burst into flame with Owain Glyndŵr's uprising. This time the attack was expected. Caernarfon town may have been raided at the outset of the revolt in 1400, and when Glyndŵr himself appeared before its walls in October 1401 the defenders were well prepared. Constable John Bolde held the castle with twenty well-equipped

King Edward I from a thirteenth-century manuscript (By permission of the British Library, Cotton Ms. Vitellius A XIII, f.6v).

The seal of Owain Glyndŵr as independent prince of Wales, about 1405. In October 1401 the rebel leader appeared before the walls of Caernarfon. Two years later the Welsh settled down to a more determined siege, aided by a seaborne force of French allies (By permission of the National Museum of Wales).

The arms of Owain Glyndŵr on a harness decoration, found at Harlech Castle (By permission of the National Museum of Wales).

King Henry VII, who eroded the barriers between the Welsh and English in boroughs such as Caernarfon: a detail from his gilt-bronze effigy in Westminster Abbey (By courtesy of the Dean and Chapter of Westminster).

men-at-arms and eighty archers — all recently paid — and the English townsmen were not at all impressed by Owain's display of a white banner with a golden Welsh dragon. Charging out from their defences, garrison and settlers drove off the attackers with the loss of three hundred Welsh dead. But the danger was far from past, and two years later the Welsh settled down to a far more determined siege, aided by a seaborne force of their French allies. By the end of 1403 only twenty-eight of the castle's garrison survived, and early in the following year a female messenger had to slip through the Welsh lines with a verbal appeal to Prince Henry for help 'because there was no man who dared to come, and neither man nor woman dare to carry letters'.

Relief eventually came, but the Glyndŵr revolt left a bitter residue of inter-racial enmity, backed up by new and still more severe anti-Welsh laws. Yet Caernarfon could not remain for ever an alien enclave, sealed off from the surrounding Welsh population. It will have been remembered that at least two local Welsh squires had died defending the town against Glyndŵr, while no amount of legislation could hinder the increasing number of marriages or less regular unions between English and Welsh. Nor could the townsmen's dogged determination to defend their racial privileges prevent the gradual infiltration of Caernarfon by Welsh merchants and gentlemen, and the Welsh-descended King Henry VII took the legal wind out of their sails by repealing the old anti-Welsh laws. The Act of Union of 1536, guaranteeing the equality of the two nations, ended the exclusive status of Caernarfon altogether: there was no longer any need for a fortified frontier town, for there was no longer a frontier.

Neither was there any need for a castle, and apart from the brief flurry of activity during the Civil War of the 1640s, Caernarfon's was left to crumble quietly into ruin. In 1660, indeed, the government decided to demolish it altogether, but nothing came of this, and as Caernarfon turned into an almost exclusively Welsh town — a process hastened by the vast increase in Welsh-speaking population attracted by the flourishing slate trade of the early nineteenth century — so the local perception of the castle also gradually changed.

By the time the artist J. M. W. Turner (1775-1851) painted this view of Caernarfon, 1799-1800, the town had become almost exclusively Welsh. Turner's somewhat romanticized view avoids the 'slate quay'. The slate trade led to a vast increase in the population of the borough, and many of those attracted to work at the quay were native speaking (By courtesy of the Trustees of the British Museum).

Its origin as an instrument of foreign domination already largely forgotten, the castle ceased to be a nuisance to be demolished and developed into a source of national pride, to be carefully conserved. The culmination of this development was probably Prince Edward's Investiture there in 1911, promoted by the radical Welshman Lloyd George to please and honour his fellow-countrymen. Though Edward was called prince of Wales, no-one could pretend he was a Welshman — despite the few Welsh phrases he parrot-learned from Lloyd George for the occasion: but Caernarfon Castle, where the ceremony took place, was widely referred to by both the Welsh and the English press as 'a mighty Welsh fortress', or 'this great landmark in our (Welsh) national history'. In the popular mind at least, then, the castle founded by King Edward I to subdue the Welsh had been reclaimed by the people it was built to oppress.

Caernarfon Castle: Initially a bitter afront to the Welsh people, but now much more a source of national pride.

Since then, Welsh perceptions of Caernarfon have to some extent changed again. One of the leading opponents of Prince Charles's Investiture there called it 'a castle built by Welsh slave labour under the orders of the intruder', a description much repeated. It is in point of fact mostly wrong, for the labourers who built the fortress were neither Welsh nor slaves: they came from thirty-two English counties (principally Yorkshire and Lincolnshire) and though admittedly conscripted, they were at least paid wages. That Caernarfon Castle was raised on the orders of an intruder, however, cannot be denied: though how great a part it played in overawing the Welsh is more questionable. Neither Madog ap Llywelyn in the thirteenth nor Owain Glyndŵr in the fifteenth century was greatly impressed by it, for the first occupied it, and the second, having failed to take it, simply isolated and ignored it. Even in its medieval heyday, then, King Edward's greatest fortress-palace may have been something of a magnificent white elephant. Now its tusks have long since decayed, and it perhaps remains a symbol of Welsh defeat only if Welshmen wish it to be so.

Further Reading

R. Barber, *Edward, Prince of Wales and Aquitaine: A Biography of the Black Prince* (London 1978).

A. D. Carr, *Llywelyn ap Gruffudd* (Cardiff 1982).

John Cannon and Ralph Griffiths, *The Oxford Illustrated History of the British Monarchy* (Oxford 1988).

Jeffrey L. Davies, *Segontium Roman Fort* (Cadw, Cardiff 1990).

Hilda Johnstone, *Edward of Carnarvon* (Manchester 1946).

Gwyn Jones and Thomas Jones, editors, *The Mabinogion* (London 1948).

Michael Prestwich, *Edward I* (London 1988).

Arnold Taylor, *The Welsh Castles of Edward I* (London 1986).

Arnold Taylor, *Caernarfon Castle and Town Walls*, revised edition (Cadw, Cardiff 1989).

David Walker, *Medieval Wales* (Cambridge 1990).

K. Williams-Jones, 'Caernarvon', in R. A. Griffiths, editor, *Boroughs of Mediaeval Wales* (Cardiff 1978), pp. 73-101.